D0290092

How to Mind-Read Your Customers

How to Mind-Read Your Customers

Using Insights from Psychology to Increase Sales and Develop Better Business Relationships

DAVID P. SNYDER

AMACOM
American Management Association

New York • Atlanta • Boston • Chicago • Kansas City • San Francisco • Washington, D.C.
Brussels • Toronto • Mexico City • Tokyo

Special discounts on bulk quantities of AMACOM books
are available to corporations, professional associations,
and other organizations. For details, contact Special
Sales Department, AMACOM, a division of
American Management Association,
1601 Broadway, New York, NY 10019
Tel.: 212-903-8316. Fax: 212-903-8083.
Web Site: www. amacombooks.org

This publication is designed to provide accurate and authoritative
information in regard to the subject matter covered. It is sold with
the understanding that the publisher is not engaged in rendering
legal, accounting, or other professional service. If legal advice or
other expert assistance is required, the services of a competent
professional person should be sought.

Library of Congress Cataloging-in-Publication Data

Snyder, David P.
    How to mind-read your customers : using insights from psychology to
increase sales and develop better business relationships / David P.
Snyder.—2nd ed.
        p.   cm.
    ISBN 0-8144-0599-1 (pbk.)
        1. Selling   2. Marketing.   I. Title.

HF5438.25 .S646 2001
658.85—dc21   00-054313

© 2001 David P. Snyder.
All rights reserved.
Printed in the United States of America.

This publication may not be reproduced,
stored in a retrieval system,
or transmitted in whole or in part,
in any form or by any means, electronic,
mechanical, photocopying, recording, or otherwise,
without the prior written permission of AMACOM,
a division of American Management Association,
1601 Broadway, New York, NY 10019.

Printing number

10   9   8   7   6   5   4   3   2   1

To Lind, with love and thanks and best wishes.

Also, to my beloved daughter, Vivian, just two years old. May your mind grow full of knowledge, your heart full of understanding and appreciation, and your soul full of tolerance.

To my parents, Charles and Marjorie Snyder, for the gift of faith.

And to Angie, for her incomparable understanding and vision of the future.

Contents

Part 2: Advanced Chemistry

Preface

If for some strange reason you run into a snag or face some kind of time-management crisis and are unable to finish reading this book, I hope you will at least get the chance to read this brief preface. It contains one of the most important lessons of the book distilled down to about seven hundred words.

As I go around speaking with some of the top corporate-education executives at some of the nation's leading companies and financial institutions, I often hear them talk about how difficult it is for their salespeople to face rejection and the loss of potential earnings that comes with it. Many sales directors who are dedicated to their people say they wish they could somehow convince their team members to stop concentrating exclusively on money or successful hits as a way of measuring self-worth. As many of them admit, money is a dangerous thing upon which to base your self-esteem. In fact, people who base their sense of worth on material success are doomed to misery—even most millionaires will tell you that.

You might think that is a strange statement to make for a book on salesmanship and marketing, but, ironically, this statement contains an essential secret that is critical to your success as a sales and marketing expert. To put it simply, you will be much more successful as a businessperson, and much richer, say many experts, if you base your sense of worth primarily on your *professionalism* and your *presentation style* and not upon your earnings. According to many wise people, professionals who base their sense of worth on their style, as opposed to their earnings, naturally attract more customers, have better public personalities and images, and are much less influenced or derailed by the inevitable rejections that occur in the business world. As both you and I know, rejection is not fun, but everyone in the business world has to be emotionally hardy enough to face it on a daily basis.

One of the most important themes I have to offer in this book comes from observing many happy and successful businesspeople go about their daily lives. From watching these people—many of whom are profiled in this book—I have learned that you must take pride in your manner, your style, the eloquence of your delivery, and the beauty of your sales presentation—whether the customer buys or not. And you must go as far as you can go, at every moment, to show as much respect to your prospects as you possibly can. Overwhelm them with respect. And be tenacious—but indomitably and unswervingly polite.

Do these things so that when you walk out of a room after any meeting, whether you make the sale or not, you can say to yourself: That was the best sales presentation this person has ever seen. I was respectful. I was eloquent. I was passionate about my ideas. I clearly explained the benefits and my sales presentation package was a work of art.

If you base your self-esteem on this dedication to style, while simultaneously learning how to appreciate and react to the different behavioral styles of your customers, people will become magnetized by your presence and they will want to do business with you. That's the central message most corporate sales geniuses would have you learn.

Having said that, we will spend the next 200 pages or so talking about the various refined techniques you can use to make your presentation supremely sophisticated and psychologically astute.

How to Mind-Read Your Customers

Getting to know yourself and being proud of who you are, in fact, is the most powerful psychological advantage you have as a businessperson and salesperson. It will also give you a sense of peace beyond Zen.

(from Chapter 1)

It's a sorry dog that can't wag its own tail.
—Often quoted by Mabel Ballagh "Ne Ne" Snyder (author's grandmother), 1904–1987

Introduction

The premise of this book is rather simple. For almost a decade now I have had the opportunity to observe, talk with, and interview some of the world's greatest salesmen—including the chief executive officers and top-ranking executives of some of the world's most powerful corporations, along with leading entrepreneurs. I have learned a lot from these master salespeople and I am going to share what they have taught me about the art of selling.

Recent events have confirmed my belief that mastering the art of salesmanship is an important and worthwhile path of knowledge for anyone to pursue.

Because of my background, other companies and business-education centers began to ask me to conduct training seminars on the psychology of salesmanship. The idea fascinated me at first, so I enthusiastically accepted those early offers. And I am glad I did.

After conducting my first few seminars, I knew that I had a useful product because participants were writing or calling to tell me that my seminar, How to Mind-Read Your Customers, was the best seminar on salesmanship they had ever attended, and that the lessons I had shared had helped them to dramatically increase their sales efforts.

Therefore, I decided to take the seminar and put it in the form of a book—and that is what you see here.

I began my intensive education in the art of master salesmanship at the age of twenty-eight when I accepted the job of senior editor of *LEADERS* in New York, a magazine predominantly read by and written by CEOs and other world leaders.

As I got to know many of the world's top executives, either on

1

the telephone or through personal meetings, it began to dawn on me that all of them were master salespeople, and that they all used a precise formula for communicating with the public.

If I can point to one common trait that all master salespeople and corporate leaders seem to have in common, it is this: Great salespeople have a brilliant ability to make every valuable or potentially valuable person they meet feel like the most important person in the world.

They seem to share other traits as well. This first one might come as a shock, but it is true. Most powerful leaders and master salespeople come across as being extremely modest and humble.

Whether they really are humble might be hard to determine—perhaps some are merely good at faking humility—but the point is most people who have truly made it project an aura of calm and modest self-confidence.

I will never forget the day I got the chance to interview Richard Branson, chairman of the Virgin Group of companies, and founder of Virgin Atlantic Airways and Virgin Records, among other enterprises. Needless to say, Branson is one of the most successful and wealthy businesspeople in Europe, a bona fide marketing genius if there ever was one.

I expected Branson to arrive at the offices of *LEADERS* in the back of a limousine accompanied by an entourage. My expectations were wrong. His secretary called me fifteen minutes before the interview to say that Mr. Branson was walking over from his hotel on Avenue of the Americas.

Sure enough, he showed up at our office on foot, wearing casual shoes and a simple pullover sweater. When I met him in our lobby, he was quietly checking out the photographs of world leaders hanging on the walls.

During the next two hours, he never checked his watch once. He was relaxed and unhurried and indicated that he could stay "as long as it takes." Then he proceeded to outline his ideas on the future of the European economy.

When the interview was over, he modestly shook hands all

around and then casually strolled back out into the city, walking to his next appointment.

He didn't have a cell phone. He didn't have a pager.

And he makes more money than almost any other entrepreneur in Great Britain, the last I heard.

Branson is a master salesman. He has no need to put on a show because he knows exactly who he is, and he's perfectly comfortable in his own skin. He has absolutely no pretensions, as far as I can tell, and he's a completely regular guy. But he's also very skillful at getting other people to support his ideas.

Throughout the book I will reiterate the main psychological strengths that Richard Branson and other superrich—and super-nice—people like him seem to have in common. It is my impression that these psychological strengths can be cultivated.

There are two key themes that I will be talking about simultane-ously—the principles of salesmanship and the principles of psychol-ogy in business.

I have already explained my first exposure to great business-people.

My most riveting exposure to the "cutting edge" of behavioral psychology came when I decided to pursue a master of liberal arts degree in psychology at Harvard University's Extension School. I was fortunate enough to be invited to help conduct research at the Mind/ Body Medical Institute of Harvard Medical School, under the super-vision of Dr. Gregg Jacobs of Beth Israel Deaconess Medical Center/ Harvard Medical School, who works closely with Dr. Herbert Benson, the legendary pioneer of behavioral medicine.

Under Dr. Jacobs I helped to conduct a series of studies investi-gating the link between brain-wave patterns and emotional styles. This experience revealed to me that every human personality is as unique as a fingerprint—and, of course, this opportunity to partici-pate in scientific research greatly accelerated my continuing fascina-tion with behavioral psychology, a subject that I believe is extremely important to the integrated service of salesmanship, marketing, and customer service.

All of this said, here is an overview of the most important themes of this book:

- *Salesmanship is a science and a philosophy.* The more you learn about the science of selling, the better you become at it.

- *Salesmanship is about finding your true and most powerful self and becoming truly proud of who you are.* The more you project a calm but unshakable self-confidence, the more people will want to buy from you.

- *Salesmanship is about becoming a better person.* Master salespeople have learned to identify their strengths and weaknesses, and they have learned to control their weaknesses and build upon their strengths. They also have learned to appreciate the strengths and weaknesses of other people.

- *Salesmanship is about the intense study of humanity and psychology.* Realize that there's roughly a 75 percent chance that the next person you meet will not have the same behavioral style or pet peeves that you do, if you accept the useful notion that people generally fall into four different behavioral categories, as described in this book. If you do not recognize what kind of person you're about to sell to, you stand a very good chance of saying something that will push all the wrong buttons and destroy your chances of making a successful sale.

- *Salesmanship is about having more fun in life.* Great salespeople have a fresh and eternally youthful outlook on life. They wake up every morning flooded with an exuberant sense of opportunity to make the most out of life, have fun, be nice to people, and get rich. And they realize there's absolutely nothing in the world wrong with that because, just like Benjamin Franklin, they know that God helps those who help themselves.

- *Salesmanship is all about karma.* What goes around comes around. Might sound corny, but you'll never achieve your maximum success until you grasp the meaning of this fundamental concept. It essentially means that you are supposed to be enthusiastic and excited about life, opportunity, and learning, especially if you want to be a successful businessperson. It also means that you have to want to leave the business world a better place than you found it.

Aside from these, there is one final idea that I want you to focus on as you work your way through this book: *integration.*

Simply put, most leading companies have come to realize that customer service, sales, and marketing are not separate functions but are one and the same—three corners of a triangle. Yet if you were to attempt to ask the marketing or sales geniuses interviewed in this book to describe their specific *strategy* for achieving this integration, you might get a blank stare: Many of them simply don't understand why other people see a separation in the first place.

To all of the sales and marketing leaders represented in this book, sales, marketing, and customer service are based upon a fundamental knowledge of relationships intermingled with a genuine fondness and respect for other people. In fact, every single one of the top sales or marketing people in this book, as either observed by myself or their close associates, shares one fundamental trait with the others: All have a phenomenal ability to make friends quickly and to build long-lasting and profoundly deep human relationships based upon trust, confidence, reliability, and steadfastness. They are not fair-weather friends.

Now here is the important part—these masters of sales and marketing use the very same techniques for building relationships with their customers that they use to build long-standing relationships with their personal friends. Then, they inevitably go on to teach their own companies how to use the same values to build relationships with other companies and create an even wider customer base. Because of this underlying philosophy regarding the utmost importance of genuine, lasting, and trust-based relationships, the master marketing and sales geniuses I know don't have the mental ability (thank goodness) to see a separation among customer service, sales, and marketing. In the minds of great sales and marketing people, these concepts have always been integrated.

So, although I have asked several top marketing and sales experts to attempt to explain—step by step—their integration strategy for customer service, sales, and marketing, I feel that the best way to learn what they do well is to listen carefully to their life stories, which have been scattered throughout this book. The theme of integration is imbedded in almost every observation they have to offer.

By paying careful attention to the genuine ethics, values, and people skills of the leaders represented herein, I think all of us can learn a lot about the defining qualities of real sales, marketing, and customer service leadership in the marketplace today.

PART 1
Basic Formulas

CHAPTER 1

Salesmanship as an Art and a Science

There is an easy way and a complicated way of talking about the art of selling, just as there is an easy way and a hard way to live.

Since I personally like books that are easy to understand, I will try to present things as simply as I can. But since I know some of us also enjoy the theoretical, difficult, and mentally challenging aspects of marketing theory, I will throw in a little bit of that, too.

First, the simple stuff.

One of the things that I have liked the most about interviewing executives and CEOs is that on many occasions I have had to sit patiently in the corner of a large office while the executive took a sales call that could not be missed. Listening to these sales calls has been an education in itself.

The funny thing is, almost every salesperson I have ever heard on the phone uses exactly the same approach. It is not like the movies, such as in Oliver Stone's *Wall Street,* where high-powered egomaniacs are talking fifty million miles an hour into their cell phones and screaming at the top of their lungs to convince people to buy their products or ideas.

In fact, what you hear is exactly the opposite. Most buyers, whether those buyers are elderly people looking for a good vacuum cleaner or a board of directors looking for a new CEO, are cautious buyers, and they tend to trust soft-spoken, highly credentialed people who talk slowly, express the facts, and give other people time to think.

This is how real master salespeople act:

- Master salespeople, especially when they are on a sales call, either in person or on the phone, speak very quietly and very slowly.

- Master salespeople on a sales call hardly ever seem to show any emotion except for enthusiasm, compassion, or positive regard. They never display prejudice, political opinions, or any kind of defensiveness or negative emotion whatsoever. Master salespeople rarely get angry and *never* express anger, even if they feel it.

- Master salespeople never take no for an answer but always seem to quietly find some different angle to pursue in conversation, even if their original proposal is turned down.

- Master salespeople seem to always find a way to get every caller to "leave the door open" for another conversation, even if they don't get what they want the first time.

- Master salespeople seem to realize that cultivating and building personal relationships is more important than making an immediate sale. They would never compromise a friendship to make a sale. But by using this approach, they make more sales to more people more often.

Those are the basic similarities I have noticed about all master salespeople whenever I have seen them in action in person or on the telephone.

But there is another important similarity I have noticed that is harder to capture in a few phrases. It is this: Most master salespeople seem to use a precise scientific formula to communicate themselves and their products to potential customers in an extremely methodical but powerful fashion. After listening to many master salespeople do the same thing several thousand times, I began to figure out what they were doing.

I gradually discovered that they were all using an invisible marketing worksheet that contained a highly distilled and focused strategy for communicating certain key points about themselves and their products to every person they talked with. They all seemed to have done research on the personality styles and the interests of the people to whom they were trying to sell. And they used a different style of communication, depending on whom it was they were talking to.

Moreover, I noticed that all these master salespeople almost always spoke in a level, nonemotional tone in short, direct sentences. And although each one used a highly personalized technique, they were all using some kind of invisible sales sheet in their heads that might look something like this if you were to put it on paper:

Sales Strategy Worksheet

Customer: _____ Time/Date: _____ Assistant(s): _____

Telephone: _____ Fax: _____ E-mail: _____

Address: _____

Occupation of customer/buying power: _____

Product to sell this customer: _____

Competitive strengths of my product:

1. _____
2. _____
3. _____

What's in it for the customer? Why should the customer care about my product?

1. _____
2. _____
3. _____

Customer type:

Age/Sex/Marital status/Education: _____

Personality type: _____

Stress points: _____

Calming points: _____

Interests/Family values: _____

Sales strategy: _____

Initial comments of customer to first call and follow-up strategy: (i.e., How did I handle obstacles and what do I plan to do. . . . keeping notes on every call) _____

Granted, all master salespeople, such as CEOs and other top executives, don't actually have paper versions of this kind of worksheet. Some simply carry the information around in their heads. But make no mistake about it, all master salespeople know every single piece of information that would be included on such worksheets, if they used them. And some of them actually do.

So, in the first part of the book we will spend some time talking about why it is important to know each piece of information on this Sales Strategy Worksheet; then, in the next part, we will talk about how to use this information to your sales advantage once you have it.

But first, I want to introduce you to another "invisible sheet" that all master salespeople seem to use. Let's call it the Marketing Identity Worksheet. It is this sheet that gives the master sales and marketing professional that supreme self-confidence and power in a sales call. It is each businessperson's manifesto, and it guides every business letter, marketing statement, or press release he will ever write or approve.

If you were to put the key elements of this invisible Marketing Identity Worksheet on one page, it would look something like this:

Marketing Identity Worksheet

Company name: _____

My mission: _____

_____

My values: _____

_____

Services and/or product(s): _____

Potential customers: _____

Competitive strengths of services and/or product(s):

1. _____

2. _____

3. _____

What's in it for the customer? Why should the customer care what I have to say?

1. _____

2. _____

3. _____

Now, anyone who has completed a few business courses might scoff at such a sheet, protesting that it is too simplistic.

Only after they have been successful in business for a while or have accepted tenure as a professor at a major business school does it dawn on most people that marketing *is* simple and that if you ignore the basics for one second, you're finished before you start.

That is why every single CEO or other master salesperson I have ever met seems to project with absolute solid authority, every single second spent in public, the filled-in blanks of the Marketing Identity Worksheet.

As a matter of fact, to continue refining the message of their key marketing points and then commit the message of this worksheet to heart and memory until it becomes a mantra is usually an ongoing and pivotal part of their job. To keep selling this refined message to the entire organization is the next step.

Why?

Think about it. The preparation that goes into a sale may take months and months of intellectual analysis, but there always comes the moment of truth that, for lack of a better expression, is called the sales call.

The sales call might be a presentation made before a corporate board, or it might be an interview on someone's front porch. It doesn't matter. The approach has to be the same. You don't have the time or the luxury to make up your sales presentation on the spot. If you try to wing it, most people will think you're unprofessional, or simply mad.

The business world has no tolerance for extemporaneous genius or sudden bursts of wild emotion and undisciplined enthusiasm.

In business, you must always project yourself as being nonemotional, well-prepared, and *right,* just like *Star Trek*'s Mr. Spock. *Most* potential buyers, because of the science of personality, would buy anything from Mr. Spock, because Mr. Spock has no emotions—just facts. As mentioned, most buyers, as a general rule, are made suspicious by high emotion and uncontrolled enthusiasm.

On the other hand, buyers *are* made comfortable by facts and a calm assurance: "My product is going to take the guesswork and uncertainty out of your life."

Therefore, your sales pitch has to be memorized; it has to be precise; it has to include a personal knowledge of all the information on the worksheet above; and whether you like it or not, it has to be *spiritually oriented.*

By spiritually oriented I mean this: *You must be selling a product that you believe in to the core of your soul,* and that you feel can make people's lives better, or easier, or ease human suffering in some way.

If you do not feel this passionately about your product, no one is going to buy it. Even worse, people will sense your insecurity and will resent you for trying to sell something you don't believe in, and your reputation will be ruined forever with these people.

Now, some people might challenge this idea, saying that it is not applicable if, for example, you are selling garden seeds or used cars. It is my experience, however, that the spiritually grounded and customer-conscious aspects of sales are paramount, no matter what you are selling—even if it *is* used cars. The reason is that, again, most people are made uncomfortable by people who give potential clients or customers the impression that they are selling something they do not believe in, and/or that they might be trying to sell them something that they don't need or want. Your ultimate goal as a salesperson is to put people at ease and to let them know that you are concerned about their purchase. So even if you are selling used cars, you will sell a lot more of them if you make a habit of letting your customers know that you do not want to sell them a used car that is not right for them, and that you would like to make the extra effort and take the extra time to help them find something that best suits their needs.

Rule: The most important thing you can do as a businessperson and a salesperson is to convince other people that you have an almost religious dedication to and belief in your company and the value of its products to improve the quality of human life and happiness as well as a devotion to a cause.

That is why it is important to make very sure that you have correctly filled in the Marketing Identity Worksheet before you go out on a sales call or get on the phone and attempt to sell your company, an idea, a product, or a service.

Therefore, let us look at the elements of that Marketing Identity Worksheet one by one and talk about why they are important.

Your Company Name

Your company name had better be good, especially if it is a new company. It is your primary sales tool. It should be short, powerful, and have a lofty, service-oriented ring to it. A name that you can feel truly proud of.

A great company name, in my opinion, is ICon, the name of the computer service and Internet corporation with offices located in New York and New Jersey. At the time this book was written, my good friend Tom Livaccari was vice president of New Media for ICon and was serving on the advisory board of my own company. (Tom has since moved on to become director of sales and marketing for Dennis Interactive, one of the nation's leading Interactive software development companies and a subsidiary of Dennis Publishing, the largest independently owned publishing company in the United Kingdom. A master salesman, Tom will present his theories on the psychology of salesmanship in Chapter 11.)

Not only does the name ICon connote the "paragon of authority," it is also linked with one of the most visible and often-used symbols in software, that of the computer software program *icon.*

And there's a lot more going on in the ICon name, too. Remember that a few paragraphs before I said that all great business visionaries have tried to find a way to project their companies as having an aura of almost religious integrity and devotion to a cause.

Please do not underestimate the importance of having such an aura around your company.

Look, for example, at the definition of icon from the Random House Dictionary: "*Icon N. 1.Eastern Ch.* representation of a sacred personage . . . ; 2. anything devotedly admired."

Now, it is easy to see that, with such a name, any person calling on behalf of this company has a distinct psychological advantage. Their psychological advantage is that they are portraying themselves as being associated with things that are:

1. Sacred, or treated as sacred by the people who work for it

2. Unquestionably authoritative

3. Admired by everyone else

4. Associated with one of the most commonly used words in computer software terminology

As common sense would dictate, if you are striving to come up with a company name, it is often smarter to strive for a powerful, dignified and important-sounding name rather than a cute or clever name, which, even if it works, might fade from the public imagination in a couple of years.

In some rare cases, of course, there will be times when a cute or clever name will suit your needs just fine. Say, for example, that you live in Vermont and make muffins. One day it occurs to you that you want to start your own company and you decide to name your company the Moon Patch Muffin Company. (Since I just made this name up, I apologize to anyone who might actually be using it unbeknownst to me.) All of your friends love the name and you feel good about it, too. Who knows, the Moon Patch Muffin Company name may eventually work its way into the collective heart of America and you might end up a billionaire.

But more often than not, the choice of a cute or clever name is risky because these names are prisoners of fashion and the fickleness of trends. Fashion is a very fickle goddess, and she rules her kingdom hand in hand with her equally fickle sister, Fame. One minute you are their favorite person and the next thing you know, you have been banished from the kingdom forever.

If you don't believe my point of view on this, just go into the grocery store and look at the latest lineup of supercool sodas, juices, and bottled waters. Then go back to the store a year later and see how many of them are still on the shelf.

My point is that if you are starting your own company and have the luxury of choosing your own name, you had better pick a name you can be comfortable with for a long time. When it comes to creating an image, most CEOs would tell you this: Be wary of being cool. What is hip this year will not likely be hip next year. You may be stuck with the unpleasant task of having to peel off your own skin in order to shed a name or concept that you no longer want to be associated with.

So first of all, try to associate yourself with a name, concept, and product that you are proud of and believe that you can remain proud of for a long time.

Next you must convince people that you are not only *proud* of your company but that you also *believe* in your company.

Which brings us to the next question.

What is it that you believe in?

Your Mission

There are few companies in existence today that have not devised a *mission statement* and a *values statement.*

Unfortunately, some of these mission and values statements sound patently phony, and so they have the opposite of the intended effect.

Consider this facetious example:

Big Bob's Nuclear Bomb Discount House: Mission Statement

Our mission is to offer quality nuclear armaments to psychotic terrorists and other world leaders along with the latest variety of biological weapons. We promise quality results and unsurpassed excellence with all of our instruments of mass destruction. Along with quality customer care and a dedication to excellence, we seek to promote excellent community relations and a respect for the environment, with a special level of compassion for the rights of women and minorities, except in those instances when our clients want to blow them up.

The point that I am trying to make is that mission statements have become so formulaic that they all sound alike, and no one believes them anymore, so easy is it to spew out a paragraph of pure mental garbage as is represented in the words of the example given above.

The original intent of mission statements, I think, was to get companies and executives to actually ponder what it is they believed in and wanted to do to make the world a better place—what they *really* believed in, and not what they just *said* they believed in.

What Do Mission and Values Really Mean?

All of this mission and values stuff really started taking off in 1994 when two business school professors, Gary Hamel and C. K. Prahalad, wrote a book called *Competing for the Future* in which they introduced "core competencies," a term that has now become commonplace in the business world.

I believe Hamel and Prahalad have written a very useful and intelligent book, but when you really get down to it, what they asked companies to think about was actually a very simple series of questions:

What is it that we do?

What are we good at?

What skills and services make us unique?

Why should anybody care what we have to say about anything?

With the changes that are occurring in consumer demands, what will make people think we are the best at what we do five or ten years from now?

What Hamel and Prahalad also suggested was that every employee of every company must be able to answer a similar set of questions. The most important questions employees must ask themselves might be summarized this way:

What is it that I do?

What am I especially good at?

What skills and services make me unique?

Why should anybody care what I have to say about anything?

With changes occurring in my field of expertise, why would anybody want to continue employing me five or ten years from now?

What executives, corporate visionaries, and managers are supposed to be responsible for, in effect, is making sure that the company knows all of the answers to the company questions and that each employee has adequate personal answers, which are at least vaguely related to the answers the company gave.

Obviously, if a company cannot answer the simple questions listed above, it has no business being in business. And just as obviously, if an employee cannot answer the questions that pertain to employees, the employee had better start looking for a new line of work.

But you will be surprised what many management professionals found when they began going around asking executives what their company was best at. Hard to believe, but many companies simply do not know or cannot express in the English language what it is that makes them more interesting or valuable than the next guy. I know because I have been one of those consultants companies have called upon to help define such things as "core competencies."

I keep noticing, by the way, that almost every time I pick up the paper, I find that yet another large company has "right-sized" or "downsized" and has laid off another group of 5,000 people.

Is it possible that all this downsizing in the United States is occurring, at least in part, because no one in these companies knows exactly what it is they're trying to sell, and why anyone should care? Could it be that someone at these companies might want to try writing a mission statement that actually makes sense?

Mission statements should not be complicated, but they should be carefully thought out and they should be as sincere as you can make them. They cannot be glib but must involve a certain amount of genuine soul-searching.

If you are going to be successful at marketing or sales, you must also do a little soul-searching of your own.

These are the main questions successful people seem to ask themselves:

What do I really want to do with my life and talent?

If I am not doing what I want, why am I not doing it?

What obstacles can I remove so I can do what I want?

Am I creating a personal mission statement that makes me happy, or one that merely sounds good to people I want to impress?

How can I condense my personal goals in life—what I want to achieve and can achieve—into as many words as would fit on the back of a cocktail napkin?

How can I wake up every morning and do several small, manageable, and accomplishable tasks before sundown that will allow me to get one foot closer to my goal, while reminding myself every second that no one's opinion of me matters, except for my own?

Which brings us to the next stage of the Marketing Identity Worksheet. What is it about your own character that you value the most?

My Values

Writing a values statement is the other part of the mission and values writing assignment most companies have asked their public relations departments to do.

Giving short shrift or inadequate attention to your mission and values statements is not always the wisest course of action, because many times what you get is a lot of mamby-pamby nonsense prettily displayed in a nice little frame.

This is how many combined mission and value statements prepared by public relations departments appear to me:

Two-Timing Tommy's Toxic Waste Disposal:
Mission Statement

Our mission is to maximize our profits and increase the dividends of our shareholders by disposing of toxic waste in a way that makes the very best of state and federal loopholes, while constantly consulting our excellent team of corporate negligence lawyers. Even in the face of outrageous demands from a meddling and self-righteous public, we will continue to put our shareholders first, and to dump our toxic waste when and where we want to, unless irreversible Supreme Court decisions force us to stop.

Two-Timing Tommy's Values

Integrity
Compassion
Commitment to Excellence
Loyalty
Quality
Dedication

I think you get the point. Many times, when we read the values statements of companies we wish they hadn't bothered to write them at all because we can't think of a single person in those companies who seems to reflect those values.

When management gurus first brought the importance of writing values statements into play, I think they hoped that executives in the corporation would actually sit down with one another and talk about the values that really mattered to them—the ideas that made them *strong*—and then compare notes to see what values they had in common.

That is still what management gurus would like companies to do—to get their executives to actually define the values that make them *strong* and then write a list of *shared* values.

I don't think this exercise is being done as often as it should, so organizational development directors tend to get excited when anyone shows the slightest interest in improving the company's mission and values statements.

I heard a good story about a consultant who was doing business with a corporation that will remain anonymous. This story will give you an idea of the general state of the union as far as corporate values statements are concerned.

The head of organizational development of a major corporation reported that she had been asking one of the corporation's top executives to give some thought to mission and values for the past year. After putting her off many times he had finally come through.

The management executive handed the consultant a dirty, wadded paper napkin. The consultant unwadded the napkin. Written in nearly undecipherable handwriting on this crumpled piece of paper was the following collection of words: "integrity? profit, stakeholder happiness, quality, vision? excellence?"

Apparently the executive had scribbled these words in haste during lunch in order to complete his thinking assignment about values. It was my impression that he did it as quickly as possible just so the organizational development executive would shut up and leave him alone.

But this crumpled napkin is now a highly prized possession of the organizational development executive. "It's wonderful," she is reported to have said of her napkin, in a quavering, emotional voice. "They're finally *thinking* about it! This company is headed for the future at last, and the evidence is right there on that napkin."

But, if you want to be a great salesperson, you have to give a little more thought to your values than the executive who composed that little cocktail napkin. Why? Because your values—and everything else on your Marketing Identity Worksheet—constitutes your psychological armor when you go on to the battlefield of business. They also come in very handy on the battlefield of life.

The Struggle of Staying True to Yourself

I don't think the hardest part about business is the work, after all. I think it's the grueling process of sticking to your mission and values and not letting anyone undermine your convictions or your belief in yourself.

Sad Fact: The moment you decide to be successful and focused and happy and emotionally independent, letting all potential critics know that their superficial opinions of you don't bother you one bit, you will have made enemies of many members of the human race, including not a small number of people who used to be your friends.

Why? Because some people who used to be nice to you as long as you didn't show them up will be jealous of your success. That's just one of those sad and pitiful facts of life, I'm afraid. The more self-contained, independent, and happy you become, the more hidden enemies you will create.

That raises a tricky issue because most successful and happy people are also nice, sensitive people. That's why they're happy. Because they have a heart. But, if you have a heart, you're also vulnerable to the envy of those people who don't have the courage to do what you do.

This gives you two options:

You can pay attention to the mad lunatic ravings of all the people who will be jealous of you for trying to be successful and happy; you can get confused about your values and mission in life and learn to lose confidence in yourself. If you do this, you will quickly turn into a neurotic and then help your psychiatrist build a really nice summer home to which you will never be invited.

Or, you can sit down once and for all and give some serious thought to every single line on the Marketing Identity Worksheet. Decide once and for all what you want to do (your mission). Write down, on the same sheet of paper, what it is that makes you great. Write down the values that you really believe in—the ones that give you strength in the face of adversity. Decide why people would want to buy what you have to offer the world, considering your knowledge and intelligence and the quality you have to offer. Commit all of this to memory. Carry it forth like a banner. Recite it in the shower when you get up in the morning. Surround yourself with brilliant, honest, and cheerful people. Make sure all of your friends and significant others understand your values and mission and are completely supportive of them. If your friends or significant others do not support or understand, immediately dissociate yourself from them and find new friends and significant others who do. Stick to your guns and follow this game plan until you achieve everything you want. Do not allow anyone to undermine your confidence in yourself in any shape, form, or fashion. Only share your vision with people who respect you. In this way you will save yourself a lot of money in psychiatry bills and live a long and happy life.

This is, in essence, what the importance of values is all about—getting to know yourself and being proud of who you are. This, in fact, is the most powerful psychological advantage you have as a businessperson and salesperson.

It will also give you a sense of peace beyond Zen.

In order to keep from getting overwhelmed with introspection too early in the book, we will leave our Marketing Identity Worksheet behind for a moment so the concepts we just discussed have time to sink in. But we will keep returning to this worksheet throughout the course of the book because one of your goals as a reader will be to completely think through the answers and meaning to every line on the Sales Strategy Worksheet and the Marketing Identity Worksheet.

CHAPTER 2

The Basics of
Customer Psychology

Learning the ropes as a marketing professional and salesperson is usually a painstaking and frustrating process of trial and error and intense self-development.

As most successful salespeople will tell you, no one learns the rules in a day. It usually takes years to get accustomed to the sophisticated strategies required for dealing with different kinds of personalities and egos.

Although I have made the following point before, I will make it again: When I speak of sales skills or marketing skills, I am speaking of skills that are required by virtually everyone in business, regardless of whether that person is a CEO, a COO, or a door-to-door magazine seller. The same rules apply.

Salesmanship is about presenting yourself and your business in the best possible light and using everything you know about human nature and human psychology to build a greater sense of confidence and trust among the people you meet.

In this sense, there is certainly nothing pejorative about the term "salesperson." When you get right down to it, any person involved in the business world is a salesperson first and foremost. All other distinctions and job titles are secondary.

But how do we begin to approach the study of psychology as it pertains to marketing and sales?

The Value of the DISC Inventory

The inventory I use as a prerequisite for my training seminars is called the DISC inventory. The method of analyzing human behavior employed by the DISC originated in the theories of a Harvard psychologist named William Moulton Marston, who published a book outlining his theories titled *Emotions of Normal People* in 1928. But Marston's ideas about human emotional styles never really achieved mass popularity until other psychologists and behavioral researchers revised them. Over the years various contributors such as John Geier, Dorothy Downey, Walter Clarke, J. P. Cleaver, and Bill Bonnstetter have worked either separately or together to create popular diagnostic instruments and training tools based on Marston's original ideas. (See Appendix A for a brief history of the development of the DISC methodology.)

The DISC methodology suggests that there are four basic behavioral traits or qualities that most people have that determine how others perceive them, especially in the workplace. These traits are *d*rive or *d*etermination, *i*nterest in people (otherwise known as *influencing* ability or sociability), *s*teadfastness, and *c*onscientiousness (DISC). The degree to which we make high or low scores for these traits helps us learn what our strengths and weaknesses are and how we can modify our behavior so that people will have a better impression of us.

Because of my graduate study in psychology, I have become somewhat well acquainted with most popular models of psychological theory. Many are very complicated and some are too confusing for anyone but a psychologist or pseudo-psychologist to explain. I like the DISC approach to analyzing behavior in the workplace because it is simple, useful, and easy to work with in group settings.

One word of caution: I am very skeptical about the power of any psychological or behavioral test to make more than interesting general statements about any person. Sometimes psychological tests can give the wrong reading of a person's psychological identity.

In my opinion, human personalities are far too complex and so-phisticated to be characterized or categorized by any test devised by human beings. Our knowledge and understanding of the human mind grows every day, but still, most of what goes on inside our heads is a mystery. Imagine yourself standing on the shore of Wee-hawken, New Jersey, looking across at the New York City skyline. The relative brightness of the twinkling lights you see on the evening sky-line would represent all that is currently known about human psy-chology. Whatever else is going on inside the city, inside every cab, every room in every apartment, every office, every person's head—all the stuff you can't possibly see or know from your vantage point on the cliff—that would represent what we *don't* know about the mind.

With that daunting thought in view, it's hard to get too excited about the power of psychological tests. Nevertheless, I have found that the DISC inventory provides a good starting point for people to see how they behave around others, and to help them identify and prevent some of the errors that might destroy their chances of mak-ing sales with people who have different behavioral styles than they do. More often than not, when people get their profile, their reaction is: "*Yeah,* that almost sounds like me, but there's a difference. . . ." In my seminars, it is these critical *differences* we discuss as a group. Using this approach, we all get to learn more about one another as human beings and to appreciate the subtle differences that define our unique individuality.

One note about *behavior* versus *personality:* I am not sure the notion of personality is entirely useful for management purposes. I am sure that some organizational psychologists who specialize in personality will take issue here and will want to debate me vehe-mently. But I do think personality profiles are helpful in the job selec-tion process if you want to stay happily employed as a state trooper, a prison guard, or a Navy Seal. In business situations, however, per-sonality mapping does not seem to be entirely useful since many experts have suggested that personality cannot be changed—but be-havior can be changed. That's why I am a behaviorist when it comes to business training.

In management, your goal is to help people *change* something for the better. All of us can learn to change our behavior for a good reason, but I don't think there's much chance of changing your personality. Most psychologists would probably admit that your personality is pretty much cemented by the time you reach adulthood or well on its way.

This points to another reason why I like to use the DISC method. Instead of focusing on personality, the DISC inventory focuses on *behavior*—what you actually do in front of other people. After all, it's the way we act in front of other people that determines whether or not they are going to like us, trust us, and buy what we have to sell.

I'd like to share with you the results of a fascinating series of brain-wave research studies done by Richard Davidson and his colleagues at the University of Wisconsin–Madison that examined the link between brain waves and *personality*. In one particular study that looked at the brain-wave patterns of infants, it was shown that many traits later expressed as approach-related behavior versus withdrawal-related behavior were present in the first year of life. The scientists, whose work gave rise to the studies I participated in at the Mind/Body Medical Institute of Harvard Medical School, examined infant children who kicked and screamed and cried the moment their mothers went out of the room as well as children who didn't seem to mind at all that their mothers were nowhere to be seen. The crying infants often had the same kind of brain-wave patterns as adults who displayed high scores for anxiety, depression, and pessimism. The infants who were more cheerful and self-reliant exhibited to a statistically significant degree the same kind of brain-wave patterns as adults who scored high for optimism and low for depression and anxiety.

My own mother has helped me see the veracity of such comparisons on a very personal level. Take, as an example, a comparison between myself and my brother Steve, who has made quite a name for himself as one of the nation's most well-respected authors on the subjects of home brewing and specialty beers. Studying and writing about the art and science of beer making earned Steve two book contracts with different publishers nearly simultaneously.

I don't know how much money Steve has earned because of his

fascination with brewing science, but I do know that he became a full-time book author at the age of thirty-five, and that his book sales have allowed him to buy a rambling farm on a big chunk of a mountain in Vermont fifteen minutes from the base of Okemo ski resort, and that the UPS driver often shows up at his door with free cases of imported beer, courtesy of hopeful beer manufacturers who would like him to write about them in his next book.

In terms of both his personality and behavior, Steve is incredibly steadfast, focused, and methodical. He concentrates intensely on one thing at a time and does exceedingly well with anything he decides to tackle. I, on the other hand, seem to get involved in many things at once. Nevertheless, I manage to complete these projects using my own techniques for task management.

When I brought this to the attention of my mother, Marjorie, she had this to say: "Yeah, I remember when you two boys were just little babies. Steve could just sit in his playpen and play with the same toy for two days and be completely content, just studying that one little toy from every side and angle. Now you, on the other hand, I couldn't dream of keeping you in the playpen. You would play with a toy for about five minutes and then throw it out of the playpen and start looking for another. If you couldn't find one, you climbed out of the pen and crawled off, giving me and your father a heart attack every time we had to try and find you."

It is these two scenarios especially that give me confidence that many important personality traits are present from birth. I have casually observed that in some large families there seems to be a fairly even distribution of siblings with the differing predominant traits of drive, influencing ability, steadfastness, and conscientiousness. The family in which I was raised, which had four children, is a classic example.

Being brought up in rural eastern North Carolina, near the small and peaceful town of Seven Springs, a picturesque community of quaint, turn-of-the-century-looking shops and buildings nestled on the banks of the slow, winding Neuse River, we all grew up with the same environmental influences—intelligent, caring parents; good neighbors; and lots of room to roam. However, we all turned out to be quite different and developed distinct and differing professional passions.

For example, among the children in my family, I am definitely the highly driven anxious one, propelled by restless energy. My brother Steve, whom I just profiled, is decidedly steadfast, loyal, and sincere. My other brother, Brion, the leader of a popular jazz-fusion band (whom I will discuss in the chapter on influential/sociable people) is without a doubt the influential, superfriendly trendsetter in the group. And then there is our sister, Beth, who, in addition to being driven and friendly, seems to project the strongest passion among us for analytical, logical accuracy and precision in her scholarship. Her highly conscientious streak, I believe, must be largely responsible for her stellar academic achievements, including a Ph.D. from Harvard.

I get along very well with my brothers and my sister and we have a very close family. What I value most in my relationships with them is what I have been able to *learn* from them by studying their different approaches to life and success. Steve has taught me a great deal about how to develop deeper relationships with people through straightforwardness, dependability, and steadfastness. An author himself, he also has taught me how to bring more steadfastness into my writing habits. From Brion, who is a consummate musician and entertainer, I have learned how to be a better musician myself, and how to increase my support system by developing better friendship skills with people. From Beth, I have learned a great deal about how to increase my academic and literary skills. I cannot count the number of hours she has spent painstakingly poring over documents and papers I have written, making many suggestions for improvement and helping me improve my critical thinking and writing abilities.

My point is, there are many places, including our own families, where we can find people with strengths and talents different from those we possess. The more we learn from others, absorbing the best aspects of their own leadership styles into our dealings with people, the better off we will be. The more we view others' differences as threats, the further we will diminish our own potential.

But to return to my original point, there really isn't much any of us can do about our so-called *personalities*. Personality, in and of itself, really can't predict success or failure in any field. However, there are some poor misguided souls who believe that personality and aptitude tests are infallible.

My friend Dr. Lind Hall, who is a podiatrist, took some aptitude tests in high school and was told by her guidance counselor to not even attempt a college education because she would fail miserably. From these tests, the counselor discerned that Lind didn't have an academic personality. One subsequent aptitude test that did portray Lind in a favorable light suggested that she become a minister's wife. The guidance counselor suggested that this career would be optimal for Lind, since it would give her the best opportunity to wear pretty dresses and socialize almost constantly. Wisely, Lind chose to ignore this advice, and now she is one of the most respected foot surgeons in North Carolina. So much for aptitude tests.

Having heard thousands of similar stories, I am not sure that classifying anyone according to a personality category would serve any usefulness in the workplace whatsoever, especially if you're try- ing to predict a person's chance of success in a particular role. Of course, I would not want to put a person with an antisocial personal- ity disorder in charge of public relations, but beyond that, who knows? When you really get down to it, the only real factors that determine success in any field are a person's desire to succeed and a willingness to increase one's skills in one's chosen area.

Personality aside, you may find ways to alter your behavioral style, especially if you thought those changes would make you more successful with other people. That, in a nutshell, is what the DISC method of behavioral styles identification is all about.

The DISC is also useful for another reason: It describes the changes in behavior different types of people display when they are under stress. This is very important because stress has a profound impact on behavior. Stress, which is the reaction of the body and mind to a perceived threat, uncertainty, or enormous time pressure, can turn a Dr. Jekyll into a Mr. or Mrs. Hyde in no time flat. But if you know what stress does to different types of people, and you know how to calm them down, then you can also put these people in the palm of your hand when making a sale. With that thought in mind, let's take a look at the basic human emotions in the workplace, as described by the DISC methodology and the various occupational psychologists who use it.

The Fundamentals of the DISC Methodology

Research connected with the DISC approach to behavior has shown that behavior in the workplace comprises four traits:

*D*rive or Determination

*I*nfluencing Style or Sociability

*S*teadfastness

*C*onscientiousness

Research by industrial psychologists using the DISC methodology has shown that most people seem to exhibit higher scores in one of these areas, although most people possess all the traits to some degree.

According to my observations, and the observations of researchers specializing in this area, it is one's *predominant* behavioral trait, such as drive versus steadfastness, that has the greatest impact on the way the person reacts under pressure and on the way others perceive the person.

In my own case, I know this to be true.

When I had taken the DISC inventory—I am somewhat shy to report—I showed extremely high scores for drive and determination in the workplace and lower scores for steadfastness, conscientiousness, or influencing style (sociability). Now that does not mean I am not a conscientious, steadfast, or sociable person. It simply means that when you get right down to it, I am most often ruled by my drive and determination.

But I don't need the DISC inventory to tell me that. ''Drive'' and "determination" are the two words people have most often used to describe me, along with the word "intense." Who knows where these traits came from. I don't really know what makes me tick, and I probably never will, but I do have a few clues.

When I was young, I had a severe speech impediment. For much of my childhood I was teased about my stuttering and, as time went along, I developed a mounting sense of frustration about my difficulty in expressing myself around others. The result of this was that I became very determined to conquer this handicap. I now have a career that requires me to do all the things that are extremely difficult for stutterers, such as talking on the telephone and being a public speaker. It took a long time, and I experienced many frustrations, but gradually, by the time I was about twenty, I had trained myself to be able to use verbal tricks to keep myself from stuttering too badly. Finally, I was able to raise my hand in a college classroom and answer a question without too much trouble. Now I only have a very occasional stutter, and I manage to speak before large audiences for hours at a time with hardly a hint of my former terrifying impediment.

As you can imagine, this life experience had quite a formative impact on both my personality and my behavioral style. Every bit of drive and determination I was born with got magnified a thousand times along the way in order for me to overcome my obstacles and become what I wanted to be.

Almost everyone has a story like that. If we think hard enough, any of us can point to a set of key experiences, or obstacles, or frustrations that helped to mold our adult behavioral style. As a result of human experience working in conjunction with inherited traits, some people grow up more conscientious than others, some grow up more steadfast, some grow up to be more sociable, and some grow up to be more determined.

In the next chapter, you will have the opportunity to think about your own behavioral style as well as be given the chance to begin to record and analyze your own behavioral profile as a way of beginning to understand the behavioral profiles of others. But first, I want you to consider a few concepts that will be important as we go along:

Every behavioral style has its strengths and weaknesses, or its good points and bad points. The DISC theory postulates that each behavioral style is ruled by a different emotional style and that when people are under stress and don't manage their stress properly, the negative aspects of their emotional style cause them to act in a way that is annoying or offensive to others. For example, the key emotion that is purportedly linked with drive, according to the DISC theory, is anger. Now, I don't know about anybody else in the world, but I know that I score very high for drive, and that if there's any emotion I have to be careful of, it's anger. Driven people have a tendency to get angry about things too quickly and so have to be careful about maintaining perspective on life's little frustrations.

When I or other driven people are under stress and not managing our stress properly, this is what the DISC theory predicts will happen to us:

1. We will become increasingly arrogant, obnoxious, and rude.

2. We will become increasingly demanding.

3. We will become increasingly impatient.

4. We will become increasingly in danger of losing our temper.

5. We will become increasingly aggressive and egotistical.

6. We will become increasingly undiplomatic.

Even though I hate to admit it, I have clearly seen such tendencies in myself, as well as in other driven people. If I don't properly manage my own stress level, I do begin to show my negative behavioral traits when the pressure goes sky-high—but, unfortunately, those kind of stress-induced mannerisms really turn people off.

Therefore, if I want to keep a good reputation with people, I have to keep telling myself that I must not allow myself to get too stressed out. I must strive to remain calm at all times, and I cannot, under any circumstances, display any of the negative traits listed above when I go out in public—especially when I am on a sales call.

No one in the world likes a driven person when he or she is at their worst.

And no one in the world wants to buy anything from someone they don't like.

With that thought in mind, let's consider another concept that will be important as we proceed with our discussion of behavior in the next few chapters.

People buy more frequently from people they think are just like them. It doesn't take a genius to realize that people tend to trust people who act like them, much more so than people who don't act like them. Therefore, if you are a highly driven person and you are making a sales call or a boardroom presentation to a bunch of highly conscientious accountant types, the worst possible thing you can do is act like a D (popular code name for the driven person). The best thing you can do is to try to completely hide the fact that you are a D and do your darnedest to imitate the style of the C.

Although it will be difficult and requires some practice, you want everyone in that room full of Cs to perceive you as follows:

- Careful

- Considerate

- Soft-spoken

- Conscientious and analytical

- Fond of blue business clothes

- Not too pushy

- Methodical

- Interested in clarifying and reclarifying every tiny detail until it can be clarified no more

- More of a listener than a talker

So how do you ever know which kind of person you're dealing with? You certainly can't walk up to your customers and ask them to take the DISC inventory. Fortunately, you can immediately tell which kind of person you are dealing with by carefully observing that person's reaction to stress.

Therefore, we all want to be students of stress because:

- Once we have figured out what stress does to us, we can learn to control our stress reactions and keep our customers from disliking us.

- Once we know what factors cause other people to get stressed out, we will eventually learn how to help calm them down, while earning their trust and confidence.

- If we follow the rules of stress management consistently, we will be much more capable selling and marketing our products and ourselves successfully.

Before we close this chapter, let's take a look at the basic characteristics of the four behavioral groups we will be discussing in the next few chapters: D (the driven), C (the highly conscientious).

Examine the chart on the next page and try to decide which behavioral style seems to describe the strongest component of your own behavioral style. The chart is based on some original concepts put forth by the various developers of DISC-based instruments (see Appendix A) and bolstered by the almost unanimous observations of my own seminar participants who recognize themselves as these types. Consider the fact that individuals who are stronger in one trait than in the others—which most people are—tend to speak a different language when compared with people who score higher for other traits. They are motivated by different goals, and they have different reasons for trusting or believing other people.

Moreover, each of the different types reacts differently under stress. As we have seen, high stress makes the driven person become arrogant, belligerent, and demanding, whereas it makes the conscientious person quiet, stubborn, and withdrawn. Based upon discussions with hundreds and hundreds of seminar participants and other sources, I have found these predictions of behavior to be almost always accurate.

Each type also displays very different strengths and weaknesses in the workplace. Therefore, it is essential that all serious professionals learn how to identify what type of behavioral style colleagues and customers are displaying. This way, all employees can learn how to "speak the language" of the other person in order to vastly improve sales potential and relationships on the job.

Understanding your own strengths and weaknesses and being able to pinpoint quickly the strengths and weaknesses of others has proven to be an invaluable resource for all executives, managers, and employees involved in customer contact.

In my experience, it is useful to break the DISC categories down into two other categories, just to simplify things even further. Therefore in our next chapter, we will continue our discussion of human behavioral types by taking a look at the two types of people in this world.

Strengths and Weaknesses of the Four Behavioral Types When Stress Is a Factor

	Dr. Jekyll *Strengths* *(When Managing Stress* *Properly)*	Mr. or Ms. Hyde *Weaknesses* *(When Not Managing* *Stress Properly)*
Driven Person	Pioneering Innovative Forward-looking Challenge-oriented	Demanding Egotistical Aggressive/rude Lack of diplomacy
	Common negative emotional style: Anger	
Influential Person	Optimistic/enthusiastic Motivator Team player Creative problem solver	Inattentive/flighty Too trusting Situational listener Poor with details
	Common negative emotional style: Overly emotional, needy	

Steadfast Person	Steady and sincere	Too passive
	Patient and empathetic	Resists change
	Logical thinker	Poor with priorities
	Service-oriented	Hesitant/inflexible

Common negative emotional style: Nonemotional/apathetic

Conscientious Person	Careful and thorough	Gets lost in details
	Objective and clear	Fussy and critical
	Has high standards	Picky and pessimistic
	Good analyzer	Cool and aloof

Common negative emotional style: Fearfulness

Note: Again, most of us are a mixture of these traits and emotional responses; however, most of us would also admit that our predominant style predicts our reaction when we are under stress.

CHAPTER 3

The Two Types of People in This World

If your mother ever told you that there are two types of people in this world, she was right—there are *dynamic* people and there are *discerning* people. Each of these types has its own unique way of responding to salespeople and sales presentations.

These categories are really my own inventions, used to provide a quick and easy method of simplifying some general principles of behavioral psychology. Remember, this is not a psychology textbook, nor is it intended to be—consider it more a field manual for using basic psychology in the trenches.

From Hippocrates to the Latest Hip Psychology

Since the late 1980s, many psychologists from different theoretical points of view have reached tentative agreement that the human personality comprises five basic traits: extroversion, friendliness, conscientiousness, emotional stability, and openness to experience. These traits are somewhat interchangeable with the four basic behavioral traits we have already discussed in the DISC methodology. The only trait left out of DISC is the extroversion versus introversion trait. It is this trait that helps distinguish dynamic from discerning people. Highly driven or sociable people, dynamic people, tend to be extroverted, while conscientious and steadfast people, discerning people, are generally more introverted.

The terms "extroversion" and "introversion," which were first introduced by the psychologist Carl Jung, are fairly complex theoretical concepts that deal with the idea that some people's libido or life energy is drawn toward objects and experience, while others draw away. The terms are somewhat misunderstood, however, primarily because they have been misused over the years. For example, being an "introvert" does not mean that you are a wallflower. Certain theories on the mechanics of the brain have suggested that people with this trait have a high level of arousal in certain areas of their lower brain, which makes them self-sufficient in terms of excitement and contentment. In other words, since introverts are more juiced up in the area of the brain that monitors arousal, they don't require outside stimuli from which to draw energy. They can be quite content at home alone reading a good book. In fact, because of this phenomenon, some introverts may find a high level of outside stimuli to be overwhelming.

Extroverts, on the other hand, are recharged by the same stimuli that wears introverts down. They generally have a lower level of arousal in the lower brain, and therefore, must go to greater lengths to get themselves wound up and excited. Because they draw energy from the outside world, they thrive on social situations. And, whereas introverts find contentment in quiet evenings at home, extroverts like to go bungie jumping or drive their motorcycles 150 miles per hour in the wrong lane. Extroverts tend to be risk takers—and there has been some evidence to support the fact that extroversion is an important trait for success among salespeople and managers.

Extroversion, at least in the psychology of salesmanship, is almost always linked with drive (D) and sociability (I), while introversion in the business world almost always presents itself in that discerning, analytical, calm, and careful side that buyers have. Furthermore, I think that these traits and differences even reflect the four-factor personality model proposed by Hippocrates back in 400 B.C. and elaborated upon by the psychologist H. J. Eysenck. To make a long story short, 2,400 years ago Hippocrates, in his usual uncanny way, identified four of the basic traits that we now believe to be bedrock traits of personality and behavior. As I mentioned earlier, today we call these traits drive, influencing ability, steadfastness, and conscientiousness. Hippocrates referred to them as the choleric, sanguine, phlegmatic, and melancholic traits. But if you look at the revised chart called Basic Business Psychology on pages 43 and 44, you will see that we are basically talking about the same thing. Which proves once again that good old Hippocrates was a pretty smart fellow. (Of course, his original theories also suggested that bodily fluids were responsible for different personalities, an idea that doesn't really have much widespread appeal today.)

At this point I need to make something clear. Despite what I might have said about the importance of drive and friendliness in sales, I am not saying that you have to be a highly driven or friendly person to be a great salesperson.

But don't misunderstand me. Although almost everyone would agree these traits are enormously helpful in sales, I firmly believe that any person who has his or her heart set on doing something can succeed, no matter what his or her personality type. Highly steadfast and conscientious people have become great salespeople. It all depends on how hard you are willing to work to achieve your dream.

Let's reexamine our table of psychological types with these principles in mind (see pages 43 and 44).

What Do We Mean by the "Great Divide" When It Comes to Selling?

Notice the "Great Divide" in the middle of the Basic Business Psychology chart. Remember that all of us are, to a point, a mixture of the various traits we have discussed, but it is our predominant trait that largely determines the first impression people have of us. It also determines, to a great extent, how we will respond when we are under stress.

So, despite the fact that everyone is made up of many traits, people really can be divided into two groups: introverts and extro-

Basic Business Psychology

Extroverts—Dynamic People

Salespeople and Entrepreneurs

	Dr. Jekyll *Strengths* *(When Managing Stress* *Properly)*	Mr. or Ms. Hyde *Weaknesses* *(When Not Managing* *Stress Properly)*
Driven Person *Open to Experience*	Pioneering Innovative Forward-looking Challenge-oriented	Demanding Egotistical Aggressive/rude Lack of diplomacy
Hippocrates says you are **Choleric,** i.e., touchy, restless, aggressive, changeable, optimistic, and active	*Common negative emotional style:* Anger	
Influential Person *Friendliness*	Optimistic/enthusiastic Motivator Team player Creative problem solver	Inattentive/flighty Too trusting Situational listener Poor with details
Hippocrates says you are **Sanguine,** i.e., sociable, outgoing, talkative, lively, showing leadership	*Common negative emotional style:* Overly emotional, needy	

The Great Divide

Introverts—Discerning People

Steadfast Person *Emotional Stability*	Steady and sincere Patient and empathetic Logical thinker Service-oriented	Too passive Resists change Poor with priorities Hesitant/inflexible

	Dr. Jekyll *Strengths* *(When Managing Stress* *Properly)*	Mr. or Ms. Hyde *Weaknesses* *(When Not Managing* *Stress Properly)*
Hippocrates says you are **Phlegmatic,** i.e., passive, careful, thoughtul, peaceful, reliable, even-tempered, calm	*Common negative emotional style:* Nonemotional/apathetic	
Conscientious Person *Conscientousness*	Careful and thorough Objective and clear Has high standards Good analyzer	Gets lost in details Fussy and critical Picky and pessimistic Cool and aloof
Hippocrates says you are **Melancholic,** i.e., anxious, rigid, sober, reserved, quiet, moody, pessimistic	*Common negative emotional style:* Fearfulness	

verts—or discerning and dynamic. I have used this condensed approach to basic behavioral psychology over and over in my seminars, and most of the participants have told me that the techniques I taught them have helped them tremendously when trying to "mind-read" their customers.

The terms *dynamic* and *discerning,* and how they relate to extroverts and introverts, are extremely valuable when applied to salesmanship. In a sales meeting, always consider that the divide between predominantly dynamic people and predominantly discerning people is as wide as the Grand Canyon. Always remember you cannot use a dynamic sales approach with a discerning customer.

The reason I have gone to these great lengths to create such a simplified approach to psychological "mind-reading" is this: When you go on a sales call, get on the telephone, or show up at some gala fund-raiser where it's important to watch out for land mines in your dealings with others, you do not have the time to sit around luxuriously contemplating the many wonderful nuances of human personality. You have to think fast. But having to think fast is what makes business fun. In fact, I think business calls are incredibly exciting because, in effect, they require you to have all the mental speed and dexterity of an F-15 fighter pilot dodging missiles in a dogfight. You have to be on. None of your senses can be dulled. You have to process and respond to various stimuli at an extremely accelerated rate.

When you go on a sales call or approach any potentially valuable person for the first time, imagine yourself piloting a fighter jet in heavy combat. A lot of information will be coming at you quickly. You have one chance to get it right or you'll be blown out of the sky. In a sales world, you always run the risk of creating a horrible first impression and possibly losing your sale. If you create a bad first impression, you'll have already lost.

So, imagine that you are entering a room to meet a stranger to whom you want to sell something. That stranger could be a CEO or other sort of executive kingpin, some person you have to impress at a fund-raiser, or even a fifty-year-old man who doesn't know that he wants a life insurance policy. Now picture yourself in your imaginary cockpit, looking through your windshield. An unidentifiable aircraft is approaching. First and foremost, your most important task is to remain completely calm, no matter what. Next, you need to figure out what kind of aircraft is approaching—is it friend or enemy? If you accept that people generally come in two categories—*dynamic* or *discerning*—then you accept that there's a fifty-fifty chance that the imaginary aircraft approaching you is your enemy, so to speak.

What do I mean by this? It's the Great Divide: Dynamic people find discerning people extremely annoying and just a little too *literal, stuffy,* and *bureaucratic.* Discerning people find dynamic people *irresponsible, egotistical,* and *frantic,* with little or no respect for the rules. Both sides are valid—but that's not the point. Typically, *dynamic* people often feel uncomfortable around *discerning* people and vice versa, so mixing these two types does not create a positive climate for sales.

In order to keep from getting off on the wrong foot, then, you have to figure out quickly if the approaching potential customer is friend or foe. Is this person like you or your opposite? If the person

appears to be your opposite, you must rapidly change your own behavioral style and turn yourself into the kind of person your customer likes in order to make your sale. You have to act like the
customer.

But how do you know right away if your approaching customer
is dynamic or discerning? It's not as hard as you might think.

You'll get your first clue from observing the person's level of activity. How quickly does he or she move around? How fast does he
or she talk? Dynamic people move around a lot, use many hand ges-
tures, talk a lot more than they listen, and seem generally jumpy, for
lack of a better word. As a rule, dynamic people get themslves involved in many activities and pastimes and grow quickly bored if
they are forced to concentrate on any one thing for too long. They
would never have made it as medieval scribes. They probably would
have jumped from the roof of the monastery the first week on the job.

Discerning people, on the other hand, would have made excellent medieval scribes. Today they make very good judges, accountants, engineers, lawyers, merchant bankers, newspaper editors, and
chief operating officers, among other careers that require steady and
focused attention to detail. Discerning people are very calm and they
listen more than they talk. They are usually described as "listeners,"
and they take everything seriously. Discerning people expect you to
say what you mean and mean what you say.

Discerning people are the kind of people who sit quietly at a
party and bore a hole right through you with their eyes, while a dynamic person would run around talking to everyone, if not striving
to make himself or herself the life of the party. At this party, the discerning person might get cornered by a dynamic person running his
mouth for twenty minutes, bragging and boasting and puffing himself up, perhaps claiming expertise in subjects that he knows nothing
about. But when the twenty minutes is up, the discerning person
would quietly clear her throat, get up, and say something like this:
"Well, I've been listening to you for twenty minutes and nothing you
have said is true. Your facts are all wrong and I can tell you're a little
tipsy. So, I guess I'll see you later." Which means never. The dynamic
person has lost a potentially valuable contact forever.

I heard a funny story not too long ago that perfectly describes the difference between a dynamic person and a discerning person. It involved a dynamic journalist who approached a famous discerning editor at a reception. The journalist, after one too many glasses of champagne, tried just a little too hard to impress the editor, who was a quiet and stately woman. The journalist was dressed in bright, flashy clothes, sporting a sequined scarf tied across her head. She'd been talking a million miles an hour all night, blabbing on and on about one adventure after another and about all the exciting stories she had covered. Finally, the bubbly journalist got a moment to speak with the famous editor and started right in about the time she interviewed a famous personality. In many more words than were necessary, she went on to describe how this interview, which was done in 1969, had really launched her career, and how she had never forgotten the great honor of meeting this famous person.

During the entire ten-minute explanation, the well-known stately editor didn't say a word. She just listened. She didn't raise an eyebrow. She didn't move a muscle of her face. She just stared at the woman in the scarf and soaked up every word, peering over the top of her half-moon glasses with unblinking eyes.

After the journalist finally stopped talking, the editor slowly nodded her head for a moment, and then, in front of the whole room, said: "I think it's really odd that you say you interviewed this person in 1969, because he died in 1968." The editor excused herself at that point and a few bystanders exploded into laughter. The journalist's face turned red.

Now that, folks, was a very bad sales call.

If you are a dynamic person who tends to get a little overexcited sometimes, and plays loose with the facts, do not go anywhere near a quiet, conscientious discerning person until you have splashed a little cold water on your face and calmed yourself down. Do not make anything up. Do not fudge the facts. If you are not sure that you are 100 percent correct in what you are about to say, keep your mouth shut.

Discerning people read a lot. As a matter of fact, they read all the time. They commit facts to memory. They remember practically everything they have ever seen or read. Do not try too hard to impress them under any circumstances or you'll be left standing in the middle of a room somewhere with egg on your face, just like that unfortunate journalist.

If you are a salesperon—and all businesspeople are in one way or another—I hope this little story has struck you with terror. As a dynamic person myself, and a person who knows a lot of other dynamic people, my wish for you is that you don't have to learn these things the hard way. You will lose a lot of contracts or sales while you are on the learning curve.

As you ponder the preceding story, and think of experiences from your own life that point out the differences between dynamic and discerning people, also ponder the following rule of sales: *You can sell to a dynamic person using either a calm approach or a dynamic approach, but you can never sell to a discerning person using a dynamic approach.* When in doubt, always sell using a calm, focused, and low-key approach.

The Dynamic Sales Approach vs. the Calm, Discerning Approach

In an exaggerated version of the dynamic sales approach, you might picture yourself walking into someone's office dressed like Donald or Ivana Trump, wearing a red tie or a red scarf and the biggest Rolex ever made. Without giving the carpet time to cool after your rapid entrance, you shake hands quickly, give a big smile, plop down in your seat, and say the following as fast as you can: "Jane, I know you're going to love this, so I'll get straight to the point. Besides, I have to talk fast 'cause I gotta fly to Boca Raton in two hours and then go out to L.A. But the point is, Jane, I'm very excited about this new product because it's new, it's flashy, it's innovative, and it's going to give your company the leading edge. It's efficient and effective and you can't do without it. It's the greatest thing since sliced bread and if I'm lying, I'm dying. But don't ask me, Jane. You can talk to MIT or Ed McMahon. Everybody's getting on board and now it's time for you to sign. Whatta ya say, Jane?"

Even though this is a highly exaggerated version of the *dynamic* sales approach, when you analyze it bit by bit, you can see why this approach will not work with your discerning buyer. Remember, corporate buyers are *discerning* types. If you are trying to sell to a *dynamic* person, on the other hand, the speech above would have been about half right.

What worked for the dynamic person with this approach is that you told the buyer you didn't want to waste her time, and you used the words "effective," and "efficient," and "innovative," words that make discerning people drool. But then you threw in a lot of extraneous junk that wasted her time. The reference to MIT was good, but when you mentioned Ed McMahon, she suddenly realized you were an idiot. And, that whole Boca Raton thing didn't do anything but make Jane think that you think you are more important and powerful than she is—which creates problems for you, whether she's a discerning person or a dynamic person. If she's a *dynamic*, that line just assaulted her ego, and now she's going to come after you with everything her aggressive ego can muster. On the other hand, if she's a *discerning* person, she now abhors you through and through, and she will never invite you back to her office again. So stay away from that approach under all conditions.

So what's the best way to approach this potential buyer? Pick up on the hints she unconsciously drops. When you walked in, did Jane seem edgy, jumpy, overactive, and very tense, or just a little bit too bubbly for her own good? Was she glaring at you with locked jaws and an icy, almost angry stare, or was she flashing a big artificial smile? If so, chances are she's a *dynamic* person—and would be either a driven person (the one with the smoldering, aggravated, you're-wasting-my-precious-time look) or an influential/sociable person (the one with the big artificial smile and the slightly facetious I-might-be-smiling-but-you're-still-wasting-my-time look.)

Now, if Jane has a big calendar on her wall with small neat writing outlining her five-year plan, and every paper clip on every document is positioned in the same place, and there's not a speck of dust to be seen anywhere on her desk, and she hasn't spoken one complete sentence to you since the moment you came in, and she's sitting very still, staring at you like a psychologist who thinks you might be insane, chances are she's a *discerning* person.

In either case, it is always your best bet to play your *discerning* sales card. It might be lackluster, but it's safe. Here's how to do it.

You enter the room slowly. You are not wearing a red tie. You have already sent a thought-filled proposal of what you're going to discuss a few weeks ago to give the buyer time to get acquainted with the material. You say as few words as possible. You act humble and speak very slowly. Once seated, you say the following, slowly and calmly: "Jane, three weeks ago I sent you a two-page briefing memorandum covering the competitive advantages of our product, along with the results of some scientifically based consumer studies outlining the advantages of the technology. I was wondering if you have had an opportunity to study my report and come up with some questions I can help you answer."

With a *discerning* person, you're now halfway home. You don't have to worry about her jumping across the desk and attacking you if she's having a bad day, the way a dynamic person might. All you have to do is continue this same logical course: Behave yourself, quote accurate data, and resign yourself to the fact that it's going to take at least three follow-up calls, otherwise known as "clarification sessions," to close the deal.

Now, if Jane is a *dynamic* person, you can still use the same calm approach. But be warned: If Jane is primarily driven, she might pull a few overly aggressive mind tricks on you if she's had a bad day. Or, if she's primarily a sociable person, she will be rolling her eyes within two seconds if she thinks you're nothing but a bean-counting stick in the mud.

Therefore, if you don't know what kind of person you're dealing with, it's best to take the discerning approach. And if you *know* you've got a dynamic person on your hands, prepare yourself for the mind games.

In the next chapter we will talk about the way these games are played.

CHAPTER 4

Dynamic People

A s we discovered in the last chapter, there are two types of dynamic people: the driven person and the influencing/sociable person.

The two types live and breathe for different reasons and are motivated, of course, by different factors. Now remember, the DISC inventory is used to establish general guidelines for improving your relationship with other people. It is true that everyone is a complicated mixture of all of these traits. Some people are stronger in certain traits than others. That is why the DISC is useful in business situations—to give you a feel for the dominant part of a person's behavioral style.

Highly driven people are fundamentally insecure, generally speaking. I know this because I am a driven person myself, and I have talked to many other driven people who have unilaterally admitted that they, too, seem to have a greater than average need to prove themselves. For a multitude of individual reasons, driven people have a profound need to continuously prove their self-worth or their superiority. In exaggerated circumstances, they project a profound need for others to view them as more powerful, more important, and busier than anyone else.

Earlier, I mentioned that I score very high for drive and that I attribute some of my resilience and determination to the fact that I had to overcome a severe speech handicap in order to follow my career choices. I've found, in my experience, that most driven people have had some sort of pivotal experience or set of experiences that accelerated and cemented their determination, which then became the predominant aspect of their behavioral style.

For example, many CEO types started their lives in poverty. I know one powerful businessman who was born on a barge in Brooklyn. Growing up in poverty had the same effect on him that my speech handicap had on me. I think almost everyone, driven or not, can point to a pivotal set of circumstances that helped define his behavioral style, but driven people seem to have been most impacted by experiences that challenged their sense of self-worth or importance. They may have overcome those challenges but, in a way, the challenges never left them—and they will be fighting some of the same old battles inside themselves until the day they die.

Ironically, most people who work for driven people usually admit they never want these driven people to change. I was talking once with an executive who worked for a CEO who was described as extremely driven, brilliant, and hardworking but fundamentally insecure—at least in the eyes of this executive. "And I hope to God he never changes," the executive confided. "I hope he stays insecure for the rest of his working life." "Why's that?" I asked. "Because as long as he stays insecure, he'll be up at four o'clock every morning making more money for this company," the executive responded. "The moment he becomes at peace with himself is the moment he'll realize he doesn't need to work so hard. Then he might move off to a little fishing cabin and leave us to fend for ourselves—and that's the moment when the whole kit and caboodle goes right down the toilet."

A great many CEOs are high Ds, and the people who work directly under them want them to stay just the way they are. And if the CEO needs someone to make him keep feeling like the most important person in the world, he'll find plenty of people in the company to do just that.

On the other hand, highly influencing/sociable people, the other type of dynamic people, are motivated by different factors. A person whose predominant behavioral trait is *sociability* is motivated by a profound need to be liked and to be part of the "in crowd." Sociable people want more than anything else in the world to be popular and appreciated. They want to be included.

While both types of dynamic people come across as highly active, edgy, and easily bored, there are some crucial differences, which are easy to spot:

> **The High D.** Can be very intense and more self-absorbed than others. Moves fast. Talks fast. Involved in many things. An entrepreneur. Doesn't waste time. Usually appears to talk most about his or her own ideas. Appears edgy, fidgety.
>
> **The High I.** Also moves fast but is characterized by friendliness.

You must be very observant to quickly differentiate between the D and the I. Both can appear extroverted, full of energy, and have the appearance of friendliness.

The I types are sometimes characterized as being "chameleons" for being a little too adaptive. Influential (I) types enjoy chatting and gabbing and appear to take pleasure in hearing other people's stories, often shaking their heads with approval, empathy, and understanding, even when they have just met a person. In exaggerated cases, an I might say, "I know *exactly* what you're talking about" and then smile and shake her head with a look of total telepathic connection to your brain, even if she doesn't understand a single word you've said.

Some salespeople make the mistake of exaggerating their sociability factor in order to win more sales. It's usually a deadly mistake because exaggerated sociability, like the kind I described above, usually leads most people to distrust you profoundly.

It's time for an exercise. Turn back to the chart at the end of Chapter 2 and give some thought to the various categories. Then try to decide what category best describes your predominant style. Although you could take the written version of the DISC inventory, I think it is your own opinion of your behavioral style that matters most, since you probably know yourself better than anyone else does. Besides, if you were not open to admitting your weaknesses and trying to change them, you probably wouldn't be reading this book in the first place.

So, after having given some thought to the categories and having tried to find which category seems to describe your *predominant* style, make an attempt to write down some of your driven traits and sociable traits in the spaces below, using the words from the table as a guide. For example, when you think about your driven side, do you think of the words "pioneering," "innovative," and "challenge-oriented," too, or do other words come to mind as well? Continue the same thought process for your sociable side. You will be able to examine your conscientious and steadfast traits in later chapters.

Exercise.   Complete the following:

My predominant style, in my own opinion, is: _____

My driven traits:

    1. _____

    2. _____

    3. _____

    4. _____

My influencing/sociable traits:

    1. _____

    2. _____

    3. _____

    4. _____

After having analyzed your behavioral traits under these categories, I want you to consider your personal weaknesses, or the negative traits, that seem to come out when you are under stress. What is commonly called the stress response is caused by our reaction to uncertainty or a perceived threat. Stress is also equated with the phenomenon of anxiety, since most of us feel anxiety-ridden when we are under too much stress.

Under stress, our body gears up for action and instigates what physiologists call the fight-or-flight response. Blood pressure and muscle tension increase; heart rate increases; adrenaline levels soar. We're ready for war.

This fight-or-flight mechanism has always served a useful purpose. When we were being pursued by wild animals hunting us while we hunted for our food, the increased adrenaline and all the other physiological changes enabled us to run really fast and climb up a tree, or to wrestle the animal to the ground.

The problem is the brain doesn't recognize a difference between an attack by a wild animal and a stack of bills or a mountain of paperwork that needs to be done. It perceives all of these as equal threats and, therefore, instigates the same response for each. The uncertainty of keeping a job, an impending wedding, the birth of a child, a divorce, a move to a new city or job, even a promotion or winning the lottery, all of these are potentially stressful situations and the body will react accordingly.

Of course, some people manage stress better than others, and what might tear one person out of the frame might just roll right off the back of her colleague. But for many people, the fight-or-flight response occurs frequently throughout the day, especially in the pressure-cooker climate of the business world.

How Stress Changes Behavior

Following are some of the behavioral traits that many people display when they are under a great deal of stress. Without going into specific detail at this moment on differing responses the various behavioral types will predictably display under stress, we generally describe here some of the common responses to stress. Later, we will ask you to display some of the responses that you might exhibit when you are not handling your own stress properly.

Common Responses to Stress and Worry

Being arrogant

Exhibiting demanding behavior

Being belligerent

Being rude

Being aggressive

Being paranoid

Being sarcastic

Other Common Responses to Stress and Worry

Acting impulsively

Being emotional

Being unrealistic about what you can expect yourself and others to do

Being disorganized

Not being a very good listener

Wanting things done your way

Not being open to suggestion

Acting extremely hesitant

Coming across as needy

Exercise.   In the spaces below, write down some of your common responses to stress.

Mannerisms I display under stress:

1. _____

2. _____

3. _____

4. _____

5. _____

6. _____

The information you have just written down is extremely valuable. That's because you have just described your behavioral weaknesses. Congratulations. Most people never even take the time to consider these stress-induced weaknesses, but it is these weaknesses that you can never display in a business environment if you want to be as successful as you can be. Also, the mere fact that you have taken the time to write down these weaknesses has just liberated you from them because you no longer have to run around being a self-fulfilling prophecy.

When your stress is managed, you can be pioneering, challenge-oriented, brilliant, innovative, and a heck of a lot of fun to be around, instead of being known as arrogant, obnoxious, aggressive, impatient, and mean because you can't control your stress. In order to be successful, try to keep a lid on things and pay attention to your behavior. You must control your behavior before it controls you.

Applying Your Self-Knowledge to Others

Now that you've had a chance to define and contemplate your own stress-induced weaknesses, consider this: You now have a clue about the kind of behavioral changes that happen to your potential customers when they are under stress. As you've probably already guessed, the most brilliant and powerful sales strategy in the world is to help your customer relax by letting him know that you are going to make his whole life easier and less stressful. You will calm the driven person down if you let him know that you realize how busy and important he is and that you are going to make his life more effective and efficient. You will help calm down the sociable person if you let her know that you appreciate and value her and that your product will help define her as a leader and make her better respected and well-liked among colleagues.

In the following chapters we will add to these suggestions by exhaustively covering all of the major psychological strategies you can use to win the hearts and confidence of all of your customers and colleagues. But before we move on I want you to reconsider the critical importance of making yourself a careful observer and expert on the behavioral changes caused by stress.

Recognizing Stress Reactions Will Help You Do Two Things:

1. It will help you figure out what kind of person you are dealing with.

2. You will know how to put the person at ease.

Why Is a Knowledge of Stress Reactions Important in Salesmanship?

1. Virtually all of your customers will be under stress because we live in a very stressful world.

2. It is extremely difficult to sell anything to anybody unless you can get him or her to like you first—but no one likes anyone when they feel stressed.

Refer back to the list on page 56. Do you notice any of these traits in yourself when you are under stress? If so, you can be certain you will see them in your customers. You must be prepared to deal with these responses to help your customers calm down, because customers won't think logically and listen to your sales presentation until you help them relax.

CHAPTER 5

How to Sell to the Driven Person

Selling to the highly driven person means facing some of the most challenging mind games you'll ever encounter. For the simple reason that most highly driven people put themselves into highly stressful jobs, you can bet that most of the time you make a business call to a driven person that person will be under stress. Therefore, he will probably be displaying some of those nasty behavioral weaknesses we discussed earlier, such as arrogance, impatience, or condescension.

You can't let it get to you. You must remain cheerful, nonemotional, direct, and firm with these people. Consciously or not, these people have a habit of insulting others when they are not properly managing their stress levels. But if you let them get under your skin for one second, you will become indignant and lose control of your emotions. At that point the game is over. The driven person will have won and you will have lost your sale. It might not seem fair, but that's the way it is. *They* are the customers and *you* are the salesperson. Certain rigid rules of salesmanship apply, just as specific rules apply to any game. In dealing with a driven person, you must obey the following rules:

Always remember that this customer always will be trying to test

your emotional strength from the moment you walk into the room.
You will only pass the test by remaining steadfastly strong, cheerful,
and otherwise unemotional.

*Driven people, because they are fundamentally insecure, need you
to let them know that you know how busy and important they are and
how valuable their time is.*

If you treat the game as a fun and challenging sport, without
getting emotionally involved, you will quickly accelerate your sales
success with driven people and be a lot happier to boot.

The first rule of any business transaction is to meet your customer's *need.* But driven people have needs beyond the scope of your
product. They not only need to know that your product will make
everything in their business or personal life more efficient and effective—especially cost-effective—they also need to know that yet another person out there in the world has just recognized their
supreme importance and ultimate high value to the global economy
at large and the fate of the galaxy.

However, you cannot show your respect by appearing the least
bit cowering or meek. They will despise you for it. Why? Because
driven people live for the thrill of the sport. They could care less if
they earn the respect of a weakling, any more than Tiger Woods
would take pleasure in winning a game of golf against a six-year-old.
Which brings us to rule number three:

*With driven people, you must always present yourself as a worthy
adversary.* Of course, there is a catch . . . you must always let them
win. You have to leave them with the impression that *they* are ultimately in control, while letting them know that you are tough
enough and strong enough to play in their league. Mind game? Of
course it is. But just have fun with it. The better you become at playing the game and letting them win, the more money you will be taking to the bank at the end of the day.

View this interaction as a game of chess, in which you play your
very best game right up until the end, but you don't dare yell "Checkmate!" At the very least, find a way to call it a stalemate. When playing mental chess with a D, the Sales Strategy Worksheet in Chapter 1
represents your chessboard. Do not leave the margins of the board

under any circumstances. The slightest deviation from the prepared speech on your Sales Strategy Worksheet could be fatal.

Now, remember your Marketing Identity Worksheet. You should have by now carefully pondered, committed to heart, and subsumed into the fabric of your soul all the information on this sheet. This constitutes your power. Stay focused on who you are and what it is you have to offer. Be proud—but remain low-key.

The Chess Approach

Checking Point

For you to refuse my product or service is illogical.

THE OPPOSITION

Beginning Point

- Your name

- Your mission

- Your competitive strengths

As you can see, your Sales Strategy Worksheet is your chessboard. The information you included on that sheet is your strategy. What's most important is that *you* created the board. *You* know all the answers and *you* know all the rules. Now, who do you think is *really* in charge of the game? Remember, the customer, be that customer a driven person or not, is never really in control as long as you are forcing him or her to play off of *your* board. All you have to do is smile and stick tenaciously to the answers you have already rehearsed fifteen million times.

The game starts at the top of the Sales Strategy Worksheet and works its way down, just like a row of chess pieces moving from your court to the customer's back row. To the customer's back row, you must have explained in clear and methodical terms *what's in it for him or her* and how and why you are going to make *his or her life* easier and less stressful. In fact, you have calculated it all so well that you are *making the customer an offer he or she can't refuse.*

Sales Strategy Worksheet

Customer: _____

Occupation: _____

Your product: _____

Competitive strengths: _____

What's in it for the customer? _____

Customer type: _____

Age/Sex/Married/Single/Education: _____

DISC: _____

Stress points: _____

Calming points: _____

Interests/Family values: _____

Sales strategy: _____

Calculate your words and logic carefully and in advance so that it never sounds like you're making things up on the spot. In that way, the customer will realize that refusing your product is illogical. This is a check. But again, don't you dare call a checkmate. You must continue to let the customer *think* he or she is still in control. If you do that, you're home free.

This is the moment in the sales call where knowing the differences between the four behavioral types becomes critical, because the next move is different for each type. I call it the invisible checkmate.

How to Checkmate a D without Letting Him Know It Just Happened

At the point of the game when you know you've subtly called check on the driven person by convincing him or her that to refuse your product or service would be illogical, egos will start to be in combat, even if the person really does want to make everything in his or her life more effective and efficient. On one hand, the D doesn't want to relinquish control by accepting your product, but on the other hand, the D knows he will have to give in to you to improve his life. On a subconscious level, the D realizes that the chess game is nearing the end, and that he or she is about to lose. So be careful.

Your final move and ultimate closing strategy with the D should be to present a list of options, letting the D know that you know he or she is the only one smart enough to make the correct decision. By using this approach, you have given *power* back to the D and helped her create the illusion that she is in control, not you.

You have just pulled a supremely clever move. In effect, you replaced the chessboard with a Parcheesi board at the very last second, thereby forcing the D to quickly adapt to a completely new set of rules. Subconsciously, the D will love the challenge of this maneuver and would never stoop to admit that he or she was too dense to follow along. With this psychological sleight of hand, you have just created a moment of confusion on the part of the D, while you know exactly what's going on. You've got 'em right where you want 'em—in the palm of your hand. So relax. And don't blow it. No matter how obnoxious the driven person might get, thrashing and blustering and puffing himself up, you have already won. It might take another couple of visits or challenging phone calls to get the papers signed, but in effect, if you get this far, and convince the D to review the options you have created, you are 90 percent assured of victory.

Another critical point: Be very careful of your word choices with the driven person. My father, Charles, once made an interesting observation when he pointed out that I sometimes use the word *love* too much when explaining some of my ideas and products—as in, "I *love* the simplicity of this, and you will, too," or "You're going to *love* this." As he rightly pointed out, the word *love* is a strongly emotional and romantic word, and it sometimes makes people in the business world recoil when they hear it. To many businesspeople, especially driven people, the word sounds irrational in a business context, unless there is an extremely good reason for using it. In most cases, you can achieve the same effect by saying something like, "I think you will find this information to be very powerful," or "I think you will be extremely interested in the unparalleled qualities of this product." You might even suggest that a customer will be *fascinated* by the information you are about to share. Just be careful with the word *love*—unless, of course, you are about to ask your customer out on a date.

Here's another tip: I do not recommend using the word *alternative* as a synonym for *option* when moving in for the close with a driven person. It might seem like such a simple thing, but it has been my experience that driven people hear the two words differently: You can see it on their faces. *Alternative* is a good word to use with environmentally conscious, sociable people, but for driven people it sounds too New Age.

You must always remember that no matter how much the D might be interested in your product, she is not going to hand over her money easily. She'll want you to work for it, just like she did. For lack of a better metaphor, the D is always going to behave like a bucking bronco taking you for a ride, so just get used to it. Read on for tips on how to sharpen your skills in the saddle.

How to Ride the Bucking Bronco When You're Selling to a D

The seminars I conduct on salesmanship, marketing, and customer service are not static. They're full of group participation, and hence, the ideas I am able to convey during these talks are constantly enhanced by the highly intelligent comments and astute observations of my seminar participants. The thing I like most about conducting these seminars, in fact, is that I get the chance to carry on conversations with rooms full of brilliant people. When everybody gets going, and people begin to share their war stories of salesmanship lessons learned the hard way, and laughter begins to break out everywhere, you can literally feel the pulse of the brain wattage in the room. Sometimes, the feeling of brain energy in the room is so intense that participants will actually call attention to it—and make little jokes, such as, "Gee, if we don't calm down in here, we're going to short-circuit the main fuse box."

This is precisely why I really enjoy and admire most salespeople I have met—at their best, most are extremely intelligent, reasonable, fair, optimistic, self-reliant, ingenious, and industrious. Instead of sitting around whining and complaining that they didn't get the raise they were looking for last year, or wallowing in self-pity because their parents never encouraged their dreams of being on the Olympic bobsledding team, salespeople go out there and make their own money, while stimulating the economy.

When I am carrying on conversations with my seminar participants, I always throw out my ideas and observations to them, just to see if they strike a resonant chord. And when the participants add new or additional insights to my program material, I make darn sure to include them next time. In this way, my salesmanship programs don't gather dust, but continue to evolve, and also continue to gather substance, like a snowball rolling downhill.

So, as a reader, you can rest assured that none of the comments or pieces of advice offered in this book are offered "off the cuff," so to speak. They didn't come out of the clear blue sky. Everything I am offering here, in terms of advice, has been thrown out to live audiences of living, breathing, voracious, hyperintelligent, and success-driven salespeople. Only those observations that my audiences have almost unanimously agreed to be true have been committed to print.

Therefore, trust me when I say that most salespeople will whole-heartedly admit that the act of selling to a driven person is just like going for a nice long ride on the back of a Texas longhorn bull. The ride—from initial presentation to closing—might take several months or a year, or it might only take five minutes. But no matter how long it takes, you must stay on the bull and keep waving your hat, all the while hootin' and hollerin' just enough to make sure the driven customer knows you aren't the least bit intimidated. Respectful? Yes. Afraid? Never.

I can't tell you the number of sequential sales calls I have made to highly driven people that went just like this:

Call 1.

Diligent Salesperson: Hi there, Mr. Driven Person. I sent you a letter last week outlining a program that I believe would be very beneficial for your company—

Mr. Driven Person: Goshdarn it! How did you get through to my office?! What the heck is going on around here?! Whom did you speak to?! Was it that idiot at the front desk?!

Diligent Salesperson: No sir. The professional who put me through was helpful and intelligent. At any rate, I'm calling to get your feedback on the proposal I mailed to you. Have you had time to consider it?

Mr. Driven Person: Listen! I'm the busiest and most important human being on the face of the planet! Even if you did send something, when would I have time to read it?! Call someone in public relations if you need a catalogue but don't ever call this office again! I don't have time to listen to schmucks!

Call 2. *(Exactly one week later. Same time.)*

Diligent Salesperson: Good morning, Mr. Driven Person. The last time we spoke you indicated that you wanted me to call you at a more convenient time. So I'm calling to follow up on that and schedule a convenient time for a quick conversation on my proposal to save you money.

Mr. Driven Person: %%%$@:":MJHGgf@#@$#@!&OI&OI&OIONKL!!!!/\%
/\&%&$!!!!!!

Call 3. *(Exactly one week later.)*

Diligent Salesperson: Hello there, Mr. Driven Person. Nice to be speaking with you again. The last time we had the opportunity to speak, we experienced some trouble with our connection, and you didn't have the opportunity to give me your thoughts on my proposal. Is today better? If it isn't, I will call again next week.

Mr. Driven Person: Didn't I tell you I didn't have time to talk three times already?! Do you have wax in your ears?

Diligent Salesperson: Not the last time I checked. I know you're busy but I also know my proposal will save you a lot of money and I've thought it out very carefully. So I'm going to call you again next week if this week is bad.

Mr. Driven Person: Next week is no good either! Don't you understand?! Are you wearing earplugs?

Diligent Salesperson: What about the next week?

Pause. Dead silence. You can literally hear the pages of the calendar being turned on the other end of the line.

Mr. Driven Person: Yeah that week is good. I have an opening at 9:30 on Monday. Call me then. If you call me at 9:35, I'll be on my way to the airport. Got it? Better yet, can you stop by? I'll give you five minutes.

Diligent Salesperson: I'll have to juggle another meeting, but I'll make you my top priority sir. I'll be there at 9:20 just to be on the safe side. And thank you.

Mr. Driven Person: Good. See ya then.

Now of course, this is a humorous and highly exaggerated example of the kind of telephone calls you might experience with a driven customer when you seek to set up a sales meeting. But despite the

intended humor, it's not *that* far off base—at least not in my experience. Making telephone calls to driven people is tough and you must
always be prepared to face a person at his or her *worst*. You can go a
long way in protecting your own ego if you simply prepare yourself
for these kinds of situations in advance and force yourself to remain
objective, cheerful, and unemotional, no matter what.

I find it helpful to just keep reminding myself that all rude or
highly driven customers are not *really* rude—they're just hardworking people under stress. Also, I constantly try to put myself in the
mindset of the driven customer—if I get a hunch I'm talking to one—
and actually make an attempt to *visualize* what his or her desk looks
like and what his or her workload for the day must be. It's unbelievable what many driven people are saddled with on the job because
most companies are quick to take advantage of their incredibly high
energy level. Often, driven people wake up one day and find themselves operating as the sole engine of energy that is pulling their department or even their company down the railroad tracks of
business.

Many times, this kind of person feels like everyone else in the
company is just sitting on their duff, sipping coffee, while she is
breaking her back to pull them along. This is the way most highly
driven people visualize themselves, when they are under stress. They
feel like they're doing it all, and no one else is doing anything. They
are not always wrong in this perception.

This is what you must always bear in mind when you experience
a moment of rudeness with a driven person. Think about what it
must be like for them. Are you coming across as yet another person
who wants a free ride? Or, are you coming across as hardworking,
diligent, and straightforward person who has come to offer a good
deal to make the D's life *less stressful*, while making her company's
efforts more *effective* and more *efficient*? If she perceives you as adding to her stress level, you're out. Some simple rules apply here. If a
driven person tells you that he's too busy to talk, he's not joking. He
is.

So for goodness sake, if he tells you he's too busy to talk, never
come back with something like, "Yeah, but, I think you need to hear

my idea very quickly anyway." Instead, always reply, "Okay, I'll call you back next week."

Then call him back, even if he screams and rants and raves and tells you never to call again. It's okay, he's just having a bad day. Then wait a week. Eventually, the driven person will admire your persistence, as long as you space out your calls and don't become a nuisance. What's the worst that could happen? Is the driven person going to call the police and say that you are persistent, dedicated, and unlikely to take no for an answer? You can't go to jail for that.

Another thing to remember: How do you think the driven person got where she is now? Answer: She got there *by acting exactly the way you are acting with her.* She, too, has had to learn the delicate balancing act of pushing and promoting her image, products, and services, pulling five boxcars uphill every day with nothing but the strength of her back, all the while trying her best not to insult the fragile egos of her existing and potential customers.

So, if you play the game right, the D will eventually sit down with you.

The Importance of the Almighty Introductory Business Letter

I would never in my wildest dreams ever call anyone to set up a business meeting, especially a driven person, if I had not written them a highly personalized letter of introduction first. Form letters and press packets do not count. They go right in the garbage. E-mail is only for friends and colleagues you know very well. If you e-mail a letter of introduction to a potential customer, you will only insult him by letting him know he wasn't important enough to get a real letter.

It's a pity that the art of writing the business letter is becoming extinct. People who don't know how to write one would be making a lot more money if they did. Everyone is impressed by a good, old-fashioned, no-nonsense business letter, and the more subdued and low-key, the better.

Keep in mind when sending your letter that anything that appears the slightest bit slick, glossy, overly personal, chatty, or glib will be filed in the same container holding the latest envelope from the Publisher's Clearinghouse sweepstakes.

Here's how *not* to write a business letter:

Garbage Can Letter

Dear Friend:

Summer is a wonderful time to think about all the many wonderful things we've seen at the beach—when we didn't have a wine cooler in our hand!—but an even more important time to think about the competitiveness of your health-care company with the approaching advent of managed care!

My new company, which is a spin-off of my last company, which evolved from another company that spun off a prior company I was associated with, has really helped all of us here to integrate our high level of skills to strategically position companies like yours for success.

We guarantee customized, state-of-the-art-approaches to statistically analyze the levels of core competency, which may or may not be preparing you for maximum effectiveness in the health-care environment. . . .

Wrong. Totally wrong in every way. Horrible. Pathetic.

In the first place, if you have never met this customer, she is not your friend. She will despise you for suggesting in your salutation that she is, especially if she's driven.

In the second place, you tried to be funny. Always wrong.

In the third place, you began to meander.

In the fourth place, you talked about yourself too much—no one cares.

In the fifth place, you were impersonal.

In the sixth place, you left the game board of the Sales Strategy

Worksheet and went for a walk on the beach. What were you thinking?

A business letter is highly personalized but formulaic. *It never deviates* from the Sales Strategy Worksheet. To personalize a business letter, run it past the customer's administrative assistant—gatekeeper—first, and then write the gatekeeper a *slightly* different version, including your thanks for his or her help. In this way you kill two birds with one stone. How?

First, you'll have made a friend of the most invaluable person in any sales effort, the gatekeeper to the person who approves the checks. Most of these gatekeepers fall into the category of the conscientious or steadfast behavioral types, which we will discuss in more detail in the following chapters. But for the time being, what you need to know is this: The gatekeeper won't talk much, but he will be very impressed if you act very low-key and carefully make an effort to seek his advice on the best way to follow up with his boss. Very important, you must remember that if you ever insult or condescend to any secretary, administrative assistant, or gatekeeper, you've blown it miserably. You might as well have slapped the customer in the face. Why? Executives are extremely close to their administrative assistants because these are the people who keep the executive's life in order and make his stress load manageable. If you insult one, you've insulted the other. The executive will hear about your behavior *instantly*.

But there's another important reason to start off your sales approach with the gatekeeper. If you write a nice, levelheaded letter to the gatekeeper in the beginning, he or she will know that you are a levelheaded serious person *every time* you call. This will prove invaluable later because, if the driven customer chews your head off on call number one or call number two, making it clear that he or she is just too busy for you, then you can always call the gatekeeper back a week later, like so:

You: Good morning, Gatekeeper. You know, when I was talking with Mr. Krankenshaft last week about the proposal I discussed with you the week before, it seemed that I caught him at an inconvenient time. Do you have any suggestions for me on the best way to follow up?

Gatekeeper: Sure. Last week was bad. It was very stressful around here. One of our mainframes crashed. I think this week is better. Let me talk to him and see when would be the best time to get in touch.

If you had never written a personalized letter to the gatekeeper, you would never be able to have this conversation. You would be completely on your own, without a clue and without a friend. But because you did, you now have a friend on the *inside*. That friend will know that no matter how many times the boss screams at you, you're just a levelheaded, sincere, and valuable salesperson trying to get the job done, so she will respect and help you.

The second important advantage of speaking with the gatekeeper *before* mailing the letter is this—you have the opportunity to ask the gatekeeper if he minds you mentioning the conversation with him in the *first paragraph* of your letter. If you get this permission, which is often granted, you are no longer writing an unsolicited letter; you are writing *on the recommendation of* one of the customer's colleagues. Of course, this should go without saying, but any time you are dealing with or talking to a customer's colleagues, including gatekeepers and assistants, you should be excruciatingly polite in all circumstances, no matter what. Any kind of rude behavior on your part, no matter if you were treated rudely yourself, will inevitably result in a loss of business for you somewhere down the line.

Both the letter to the customer and the gatekeeper must be extremely simple and follow the following nonemotional format:

Successful Letter Format

17 June 2001

Ms. Roberta Q. Public
Vice President
Acme Global Products
Anywhere, Milky Way Galaxy

Dear Ms. Public:

I am writing at the suggestion of Mr. Larry Smith to give you some information about a product that I believe will enable your company to substantially reduce costs associated with . . .

As I discussed with Mr. Smith, this product has already been purchased by many other companies in your line of business and has been demonstrated to cut costs significantly, while helping to increase the effectiveness and efficiency of all operations related to . . .

Enclosed is some material outlining the cost-reduction benefits created by this product, as well as documentation supporting its superiority over competing products.

Thank you for taking a look at this material, Ms. Public.

I will call you next week after you have had a chance to review it to discuss an appropriate time for me to follow up on this letter.

Cordially,

That's it. Anything else is a waste of time and probably a bad move. (This formulaic approach to the business letter, by the way, is appropriate for *all* customers, regardless of their behavioral style.)

Notice how closely this letter confirms to the imaginary gameboard of the Sales Strategy Worksheet. Here's what you're giving out:

1. You gave her your company name. It sounds solid and impressive.

2. You convinced her of your *level-headedness*. You didn't send your letter on purple paper.

3. You told her who you are and what you have to offer—a product that's going to save Ms. Public money, and/or make her

business more efficient and effective, while also reducing her level of stress. (Key buzzwords to be used for the other behavioral types will be discussed in subsequent chapters. We are assuming here that Ms. Public is driven simply because many decision-making executives are.)

4. You told her what's in it for her—you're going to make her company more competitive.

5. You told her why she should care—her competitors have already chosen your product and it worked for them.

6. You told her what your sales strategy is—you're going to call her next week to see if she has time to discuss the letter.

7. The ball is now in your court. You will be perfectly prepared for this meeting, if you've carefully filled in the blanks of your Sales Strategy Worksheet and your Marketing Identity Worksheet.

It might *seem* like the ball is in her court, because you are waiting for the company to give you the chance to explain your product, but if you do have a product or service that will add value or reduce their costs, it would simply be illogical for them to put you off forever. They *have* to pay attention to you sooner or later, or it's going to be *their* loss. All you have to do is remain calm and be patient, and keep following up with the gatekeeper on a regular basis until you get a chance to make your pitch.

If your letters and your Sales Strategy Worksheet are perfect, and if you follow the simple guidelines and tips that I will outline next to help you guard against any possible errors in your sales call, whether that call be in person or on the telephone, it will be hard for you to blow it.

Before we go through that, I want to make an observation regarding stress and tone of voice that you might encounter in what is known as the "blow-off" call—when the customer says "Sorry, we're not interested." Observing the differences in the *tone of voice* when the potential customer tells you to get lost is critical. One tone leaves the door open; the other doesn't. There are two basic rules:

Rule 1.   If the customer tells you in a controlled, nonemotional, aloof, and cold tone of voice, "We're simply not interested at this time," then it probably means he doesn't really need you right now. Cut bait and put your energies elsewhere for the time being. I would make a mark on my calendar to check back in three or four months, though, just to see if his tone has changed.

However, you can make one more effort with such people if you firmly believe you have been misunderstood. If you think you didn't give the person adequate information up front, simply write another letter stating the following:

Follow-Up Letter to a Salvageable Customer

Dear Mr. Holdout:

After our last conversation, I felt that I had not adequately explained the significant benefits created by the product I have to offer.

I would like to briefly expand upon my presentation in order to provide you with additional information you might find valuable.

There is substantial documentation (see additional enclosures) to confirm the fact that other companies have benefited greatly from using this product.

I will call you next week to see if the additional information enclosed makes my proposal more interesting to you.

Thank you for your time.

Cordially,

If on the next call you get the same cool, aloof tone and message, "Sorry, but we're just not interested," then it's definitely time to cut bait and check in next quarter. After all, that cold, aloof person might be on the unemployment line and a more receptive person might be sitting in the same seat in a few months. Who knows.

Rule 2.   If the customer tells you that she is "just not interested" and is screaming and spitting and hollering, then believe it or not, things look good. Be happy she's yelling.

If the person is screaming and hollering, that person is under *stress* and *something is wrong* somewhere. Something needs to be fixed. From a sales perspective, you can't ask for a better scenario. It's your chance to come in like the antistress Knight in Shining Armor. All you have to do is figure out what's going wrong and then find a way to convince this person that your product or service will keep her from having to scream and yell so much. If you create this impression, no matter how long it takes to create it, you will eventually get in the door.

When you finally walk into a driven person's office and get the opportunity to make your initial sales presentation, please, please, please remember the following:

1. **Never be late, never cancel, never reschedule**—unless you're in the hospital with two broken legs. If you only have one broken leg, come on crutches.

2. **Dress appropriately.** The way we dress when we are around our potential customers, or anybody for that matter, should communicate our *respect* for *that* person. Not fashion—but *respect*. Of course, if you have the greatest new software program ever invented and no one else even comes close, you can probably walk into someone's office wearing ripped jeans and a pair of red converse sneakers from high school. People are going to have to overlook your eccentricity. However, few of us are in that boat. But even if we were in that boat, I still think we would want to give some thought to the concept of *respect* when we were dressing for an appointment.

So, when you're looking in the mirror to examine your appearance just before you leave for your appointment, ask yourself "Have

I done as much as I can do to convey an appearance of respect, while still maintaining my own identity?'' If the answer is yes, you're on your way. If the answer is no, go back to the closet and try again.

3. Carry a professional-looking briefcase if you are appearing in person, but preferably not one that looks brand new. If your briefcase or portfolio looks brand new, it looks like you've never been anywhere. When I buy a new briefcase, I always take it out in the yard and kick it around some so it doesn't look like I just graduated from college.

4. Don't waste the driven person's time. Avoid unnecessary facts, figures, and charts. The D doesn't care. Get to the bottom line. Whereas the conscientious person will expect you to bring in examples of careful studies and reports methodically outlining all potential risks and benefits associated with your product, the driven person probably will become aggravated if you expect him or her to read too much. Stick closely to the Sales Strategy Worksheet. Try to explain what's in it for the customer as quickly as possible. Immediately address why the D should care. How will your product reduce costs and make his or her business more efficient and more effective?

5. You must appear credible and extremely well-informed. Think quickly but speak to the point. You will have to be fast on your feet. Consider in advance all possible objections, questions, or complaints and have short answers already prepared and memorized. Leave nothing to chance. If you find yourself having to make up information or answers on the spot, you will be shot down immediately.

6. Look into the customer's eyes and speak in short, powerful sentences. Don't appear confused. Do not look down or look away when you are speaking to the driven person. Other people might perceive shyness to be quaint, but the driven person considers it a sign of incompetence or fear. For lack of a better simile, the driven person is like a cobra. If he smells fear, he will strike. The best way to project confidence is to stick tenaciously to your memorized speech from your Sales Strategy Worksheet and to keep looking the driven person right in the eyes. If you stick to your speech, and memorize answers to potential questions in advance, you will have absolutely nothing to be afraid of. Remember, despite their frightening reputation, cobras are actually among the world's slowest snakes. If you stay alert, you can grab them by the back of the neck when they're coming at you. (But it's probably safer not to try.)

7. If you want to add a personal touch to your presentation, remind the D, "You are the kind of person who will appreciate the importance of this innovation, because of its power to make your business more efficient and effective." But do not flatter! Driven people abhor flattery. Stick to the sentence above and leave it at that. Do not try to bond with the D. She doesn't want to bond. She wants you to stay where you belong—on the other side of the desk. So be careful. Don't ask any questions about hobbies, friends, or family, and make no small talk whatsoever. Be pleasant, but stick to business.

The best way to avoid coming across as a flatterer is to try to consistently appear businesslike and scientific. Another good expression is: "I know you already understand the importance of this technological innovation. . . ."

8. If your product or service is truly "state of the art," be prepared to explain why it is. Ds like this expression, but don't be glib. They will expect you to back it up and will try very hard to trip you up. Whatever you do, never oversell or condescend.

9. Ask questions about the customer's business. Show an intellectual interest but don't talk too much. Also show that you have studied the customer's business in advance by throwing in some facts you may have learned in your research. For example, "I know you have been providing pencils to the world for the past thirty years. . . ." or something to that effect.

10. Give direct answers to all questions. If, for some reason, you do not know the answer to a question posed by the D, do not ever lie or make something up. Never! You will get caught and then you will be hanged. Instead say, "I don't know the answer to that, but I'll find out for you as soon as I get back to the office and I'll fax it over." Try not to say this too many times or you'll look woefully uninformed.

11. Stress that you understand the importance of results and the bottom line. Again, the D is essentially interested in results and the bottom line, so get to these points as quickly as possible. If you can show—quickly—how your product or service achieved results for a similar customer, prepare a little speech and bring some facts. Get it out of your mouth immediately.

As we mentioned, using these approaches, especially projecting efficiency and not wasting time, will help calm the D. Also, if you realize the D is out of control with stress (which happens a lot), do not push. Instead say: "I realize you have a tremendous number of constraints on your time, being as busy as you are. I would like to make an appointment to call you when it is more convenient. When would be a good time for me to mark on my calendar? How's three tomorrow? Is four better?" Remember, be calm but don't back down. The D will respect persistence, as long as it is calm persistence. And, if you tell the D you will call tomorrow at 2 P.M. you had better call at 2 P.M. on the dot. Ds remember everything. If you call at 2:15, you will significantly weaken your position.

Yes, dealing with the D is a mind game. The D will try to turn you into a sniveling coward, but you can't give in. Refuse to be emotional. Speak slowly and deliberately and get the D to commit to a time. Hang in there. It really is like riding a bucking bronco. But if you hang on, you'll earn the D's respect and, ultimately, the sale.

Closing with the D

Ds respond best to being given a choice of options so that they can prove their intelligence in making the best choice. This also lets them maintain the aura of being *in control*. Remember, persistence is key with the D. When returning calls, ask if they have had "time to study the options and make a decision." Make appointments and stick to them. Explain why the D might be losing efficiency or productivity without your product.

High-Risk "Go for Broke" Technique

Some salespeople occasionally use a hardball technique with tough D sales they are not afraid of losing. The salesperson will threaten the D's ego by offering to "reconsider the options," suggesting that the product might be out of the D's price range or budget, and gambling that the D will go ahead and place an order to prove his or her financial superiority. It's a technique you must use at your own discretion. Sometimes it works. Other times it backfires. I'll leave that one up to you.

Looking for Clues to Behavioral Style: How to Think Like Sherlock Holmes

When I was a youngster, one of my favorite writers was Sir Arthur Conan Doyle, creator of Sherlock Holmes. As a matter of fact, he still is one of my favorite authors. What I like most about the Sherlock Holmes stories is that they teach you how to be more observant about the small details that give you clues to a person's character or identity. Such an attitude of mental sleuthing can be extremely important when you are visiting the office of a potential client, for the objects in a person's office oftentimes give away distinct clues as to what is important to that person.

When you walk into a potential client's office and begin looking for clues that will help you on your sales call, keep the following questions in mind: What does the person seem to base his or her sense of identity on? What seems to be the measure of the person's self-worth?

Highly driven people are fueled by a need to have a sense of power or importance. Therefore, in a highly driven person's office you will often find photographs of him shaking hands with famous people, or framed letters from famous people, or you will see diplomas on display from prestigious universities, or trophies, or framed documents or awards he has received. When you are visting the offices of influential/sociable people, you'll often see evidence of their friendships and relationships with other people: photographs of their family members and friends or commendations they have received from civic groups or charitable organizations. The difference is extremely important.

Driven people need to be perceived as powerful and important;

sociable people want to be perceived as well-liked and part of the "in crowd." Knowing what each type of person needs in order to feel emotionally satisfied during the course of a sales conversation is extremely important because it is the climate you establish in the tone of your conversation that helps to establish the sense of rapport between you and your client.

Write down the major physical clues you observed on a recent sales call to a tough customer. First jot down what you remember seeing in the office, and then record what behavioral traits these clues indicated. Then, go through the same process for yourself and your own office—and your own identity.

Customer Personality Worksheet

Customer: _____

Title: _____

Buying power: _____

Chief objects of interest in office:

1. _____

2. _____

3. _____

4. _____

5. _____

Other characteristics of office:

_____

_____

What does this tell you about the customer's emotional needs?

1. _____

2. _____

3. _____

4. _____

5. _____

Now let's look at you:

Characteristics of my own office:

1. _____

2. _____

3. _____

4. _____

5. _____

What does this indicate about my own emotional needs?

1. _____

2. _____

3. _____

4. _____

5. _____

I hope that the information in this chapter, and the preceding exercise, have helped to open your mind even further to the intricacies of the science and detective work involved in the integrated approach to customer service, sales, and marketing. Before we go on to the next chapter, I want to give you one more useful tip about selling to the driven person: When you walk into a driven person's office, you should carry yourself like a three-star general. But just don't ever forget who the four-star general is. If you remember that one image, you'll do just fine.

CHAPTER 6

How to Sell to the Influential/Sociable Person

The funniest experience I can remember about my first exposure to the genius of influential people involves an interview I had long ago with Michael Stipe, now the celebrated lead singer of R.E.M. By recounting my humorous encounter with him, I hope to give you a glimpse of how inspired influential people work, and the incredible lengths to which they will go to test the pulse of their public.

I had just graduated from college and had my first real job as a staff writer for the *Winston-Salem Sentinel* newspaper. R.E.M.'s prodigious first album, *Murmur*—an album that had made them a cult craze in colleges and an album that would soon catapult the band to international stardom—had just been released. Hoping to get an interview with the band, I sneaked backstage after they played a thrilling sold-out show in one of Winston-Salem's outdoor music halls. Everyone in the band was extremely friendly, especially the guitarist, Peter Buck, although I found Michael Stipe to be one of the most shy and most pensive people I had ever met. When I asked Stipe if he would like to do an interview for the newspaper, he said sure, but not there. He said he would prefer to go for a walk.

So we took off. I expected to go for a short walk, but Stipe, wearing tortoise-shell spectacles, wrinkled cotton pants, and thick brown shoes, headed for the bypass, ambling along with his hands in his pockets, giving me the impression that he was embarking upon a major journey, perhaps in search of some other city or town that might offer additional stimulation.

As I followed Stipe to University Parkway, a main thoroughfare of the city, I began to get the impression that he liked to walk and that he had no intention of ceasing his walk anytime soon. So I continued to follow him, asking him simple questions: "Hey, Michael, do you think we should maybe start that interview now?"

"No, we're not in the right place yet," he repeated several times. "When we get there, we'll know."

So, facing a stream of oncoming traffic on a four-lane highway, we walked and walked and walked and walked and walked. On past the grocery stores. On past three convenience stores and a major shopping mall. On and on. Cars honked. People shouted. And still we walked. After about forty-five minutes, Stipe pointed to the dark horizon of the desolate city landscape and said, "There. Right there. That's where I want to do the interview." He pointed to the carcass of a burned-out Ford Pinto, which was sitting smack dab in the middle of an abandoned parking lot. In the distance, shrouded by mist, was the R.J. Reynolds Tobacco Company headquarters.

"*Wow,*" I remember thinking, "*What* a dramatic place to do an interview."

We climbed up on the car and sat on the roof and began talking about music and art. Michael toyed nervously with his glasses and pulled at the collar of his shirt as he tried to find the words to explain his great passion for writing lyrics. He was explaining how, in his opinion, great song lyrics couldn't be literal, and probably shouldn't be understandable the first time you listen to them. Instead, they should use images and metaphors that bombard you like the abstract images of dreams, so that you will be powerfully affected on a subconscious level. If that happens, he said, you might stand a chance of being aroused from the waking slumber of ordinary life. He was in his early twenties at that time and overflowing with the intensity of his talent.

I was totally getting into what he was saying as we sat there on the roof of that burned-out car, and just the way he described things made me feel that I was seeing the evening sky in a new light, despite the paucity of stars and the darkness all around.

But just at that moment, we were interrupted. I heard the sound of heavy footsteps in the parking lot and noticed that we were being approached by a very tall, thin man wearing a western shirt, cowboy boots, and a black cowboy hat. His staggering gait indicated that he was somewhat intoxicated and he was clutching a half-empty fifth of Jack Daniels.

The man stopped in front of the car, looked at us for a moment, then pointed his finger at Stipe and said, "Hey I know you. You're that guy what sings with the Police."

"No sir," the lead singer of R.E.M. said softly. "That's not me, man. That's somebody else."

The man squinted and scratched his head under his hat and then said: "Nah, wait a minute. I know who you are. My boy's got a picture of y'all hanging up in his room at the trailer. You're the guy what sings with that band the Doo-ran Doo-ran."

"No sir," the artist repeated. "That's not me either."

Now the cowboy was frustrated. He scratched his chin, stared really hard, and then tried his luck again. "Okay. I got it. You're that guy what sings with that band called the R.P.M."

"Close," Michael said. "We're actually called R.E.M.—but yeah, that's me."

"Heck yeah, I knew it," the man said, taking off his hat and coming closer to extend his hand. "I don't believe it. Here I am talking to the singer of the R.P.M. My boy's gonna have a pure-tee conniption fit when I tell him this."

Without any further ado, the cowboy began recounting the story of his entire life's journey, and how rock 'n' roll had figured into it along the way. He said that he started off being an Elvis Presley fan, but then he broke up with his first wife and got depressed, so he lost faith in Elvis Presley and the whole upbeat message of rock. This passage in his life, he said, caused him to travel across America in search of himself. He sold all his possessions and hitchhiked his way to Alaska, where he hoped to work on the pipeline. During his journey, he became a Grateful Dead fan until, "The Lord came to me in a dream and told me to start listening to country and western."

By the time the man had reached Alaska and found a job working on the pipeline, he had started listening to punk rock. But then the Lord came to him in another dream and told him that punk rock was a dead-end road and told him to start listening to Elvis again.

"I got down on my knees and prayed to God to help me find the way back," the cowboy said. "And you know, I got the strangest feeling that the King was up there, too, and he could hear every word I was saying. And the King was calling me home. So that's when I started listening to my old Elvis records again. That's when I got the calling—that's when I knew that Elvis was really the King just like they said, and Elvis was up there in heaven singing to the Lord, every day. Once I knew that, I came back to Elvis. And I ain't turned my back on him since."

About five minutes into this story, Michael Stipe did something that blew my mind.

He reached into his pants pocket and pulled out a little dime-store wire-bound notepad along with a Bic pen. "Why don't you climb up here with us and start that story over from the beginning," he said. "I'd like to write it down if you don't mind."

The man grinned from ear to ear. "Sure, be proud to," he said, and he climbed right up and sat down on the roof of the car with us and extended his bottle of Jack Daniels. We politely declined, but he took himself a good snort and then started his story over from the beginning.

The story went on for about an hour, during which time Michael Stipe filled up his entire little notepad with things the cowboy said. When it was all over, Michael signed his name on one little sheet from his dime-store notepad, and then he wrote a brief note to the man's son. The man tucked the note into his shirt pocket and shook hands with us about ten times each before setting off on his own wobbly journey back into the darkness from which he had emerged.

But just before he was out of sight, he called out through the pitch-black night with one last piece of advice.

"Go back to your Elvis records, Mr. Stipe," he called out in the night before he was too far away for us to make him out clearly. "Go back to your Elvis records and pay attention. And one of these days you'll be just as good."

After that Michael Stipe and I walked back to the auditorium. During our long walk back, we didn't talk much. We just listened to the sound of the sky above us. But I enjoyed his company very much. I knew right then that I was in the presence of what some people call the *real thing*. Why? Because Michael Stipe takes notes. He listens to other people. He values their lives. No matter who they might be. He understands that the story of the simplest people can contain the meaning of the human dilemma. What else can you say? That's why he's one of our most successful musical artists.

So take note: That's the way really successful influential/sociable people work. They listen very carefully to other people and they take notes on what they hear.

This is an extremely important concept to emulate if you want to be successful in a similar field.

In the rest of the chapter, we will discuss some of the basic psychology that determines how *influential/sociable* people relate to other people.

As you probably have guessed, I did not stop Michael Stipe during his conversation with the cowboy to ask him to take a behavioral styles inventory. So when I refer to Stipe as a good example of what I call an influential/sociable person, I am speaking in very general terms, as I am remembering his personality through the prism of time. But, even though this episode took place years ago, there are still some traits of Stipe's personality that stick out sharply in my mind. Although Stipe seemed to be a somewhat shy person, he was extremely *friendly* and seemed to have an uncanny ability to get on almost anyone's level immediately. Also, he seemed to be extremely interested in other people's *opinions* and *tastes*.

While many influential/sociable people do come across as bubbly and high-spirited—the life of the party, so to speak—that is not always the case. Some can also be quite shy, no matter how much public adoration they receive. The key traits that really seem to identify influential/sociable people are as follows:

1. They exude a quality of friendliness.

2. They are extremely adept at getting on other people's levels very quickly.

3. They consistently portray a strong interest in other people's opinions and tastes, in everything from clothing to food to music.

4. They seem to have a stronger desire than most people to fit in with the so-called in crowd. In other words, they have a strong desire to be liked.

5. They seem to have their finger on the pulse of society. They know what's in fashion and what's not—and their knowledge of fashion and trendiness is up to the minute.

My youngest brother, Brion, is a good example of an influential/sociable person. In many ways, he reminds me a lot of Michael Stipe, except that he is decidedly not shy. Coincidentally enough, Brion is the leader of a band in Chapel Hill, North Carolina. His band, called Hipbone, has attracted a very strong following throughout the south with its eclectic but highly danceable fusion of funk, jazz, and rock 'n' roll. Not too long ago, my family and I were browsing through a very interesting and quirky book on astrology titled *The Secret Language of Birthdays,* by Gary Goldschneider and Joost Elffers. We laughed out loud while taking turns reading about our personalities as predicted by our birthdays, because the predictions in the book seemed to be enlightening much of the time. We all laughed especially hard when we read the entry for April 21, which is Brion's birthday:

> *The dignified people born on April 21 put nothing above their professional excellence and integrity. . . . Because so many born on this day are trendsetters with their finger on the public pulse, they often get ahead in the world. They may lead a stormy personal life, however, with more than one marriage and many love affairs. April 21 people tend to be very sensual types, attracted to sex, food, sleep, and everything pleasur-*

*able. Their personal values are in tune with beauty and har-
mony, and their love of beautiful things . . . is highly
developed. . . .*

*The need of April 21 people to love and be loved (the
former need is sometimes greater than the latter) is very
strong and this is one reason why their personal lives become
stormy when such a need goes unmet. . . .*

*April 21 people have an instinctive grasp of power and
how to deal with it—how to control it so it doesn't control
them.*

My mother laughed when she read this passage and said that it
described Brion perfectly.

The reason I have gone to the trouble of quoting the astrology
book is because this description also seems to fit the portrait of a lot
of influential/sociable people I know.

Remember, the influential/sociable person has a few things in
common with the driven person. Both of these types often project a
high level of energy and dynamism. But the chief driving force behind the influential/sociable person is the need to be liked. Driven
people ultimately don't care whether you like them or not. Influen-
tial/sociable people care very much.

Because they so passionately want to fit in, influential/sociable
people can sometimes be a little too adaptive. Some pretend to show
an understanding of subjects they know nothing about or show signs
of immediate sympathy and understanding, even when they have
just met a person. As one of my seminar participants, a newspaper
publisher, put it, *I can be anything to anybody. In fact, I can change
my personality at the speed of light.* That, folks, is the influential/
sociable person in its most highly developed form—the complete ar-
tistic chameleon, able to shape-shift like the Native American medicine men of legend, changing from a human being into an eagle into
an antelope at the bat of an eye.

Identifying the High I

Much of the time, as already stated, the highly sociable person will
immediately impress you with a sense of friendliness and enthusi-

asm, and a desire to get to know you. She will ask you a lot of questions about yourself right from the beginning.

Most of the time, she will be wearing the latest, trendiest clothes. You will probably be able to tell, fairly quickly, that its very important to this person to fit in, be hip, be cool, wear the right thing, and say the right thing.

Don't forget about the chessboard. We still want to stay on the board when dealing with an I and stick tenaciously to our sales strategy. Turn back to pages 61 and 62 to review the chessboard and your Sales Strategy Worksheet.

Although many of the same rules apply when selling to a D or an I, it is important to throw one more thing into the mix when dealing with a sociable person: The very first thing you have to do with a sociable person is to let her know you like her and would like to be her friend—and that your potential friendship will mean more to you than business. This is the "rule of rules" when dealing with the sociable person, but there are others.

Techniques for Selling the Influential/ Sociable Person

With influential/sociable people it is very important to remember the following: *It is hard to get their attention and keep them focused unless you get on their level.* Generally speaking, too many details bother the influential/sociable person, and cause them to lose attention and become bored. So don't swamp them with details and don't get "too serious" in your conversations with them. Try to keep things light, fun, and full of spark. (I am not trying to stereotype highly influential/sociable types by saying this. In many of my seminars to date, most people identifying themselves as high scorers for influence/sociability admit that this is indeed a characteristic they share with others like them.) More often than not, the highly influential/sociable person will be glad to see you and will remain focused as long as you make a point to trade jokes and personal stories. Ask them plenty of questions about themselves. Tell them about yourself, too. Try to bond. These kind of people, unlike the driven person, live to bond. They will rarely buy anything from you if you don't cultivate the friendship aspect first.

In terms of buying habits, influential/sociable people generally tend to gravitate toward innovative, new, and cutting-edge products. So, when completing your Sales Strategy Worksheet for these customers, make sure that you emphasize the following features under the "What's in it for the customer" part:

- **Leadership.** Sociable people like to know that they are leading the way and are on an equal par with all other leaders in their field. You need to show them how your products or services will help increase their reputation as leaders.

- **Innovation.** Highly sociable people are not very interested in dusty, moth-eaten, "tried and true" products and services. They like ideas that are new, yet are proven to be reliable and effective and the best alternative. (Note that with sociable people, I tend to use the word "alternative" instead of the word "option," which I would use with driven people. In many of my seminars, people scoring high for influence/sociability have indeed confirmed that to their ears, the word "alternative" sounds less "cold and callous.")

Basic Rules for Impressing the Influential/Sociable Person

1. Don't push! Don't compromise the friendship. I cannot overemphasize this point enough. Sociable people abhor the hard sell, especially if they think you are placing business above potential friendship. Become friends first! You will have a much greater chance of selling later.

2. Make the presentation fun! Show some enthusiasm! Show some sparkle! Show some love of life! Talk about exciting places you have been, funny things that have happened to you. Go to lunch! Say nice things. Find something complimentary about your potential clients that you can praise in order to show them that they are appreciated and recognized!

3. Research the customers' accomplishments and mention them. You *should never* and *can never* forget for one second the following fundamental aspect of sociable people's psychology: Their greatest insecurity and concern is that other people do not appreciate or recognize what they have done to help other people and to promote their companies. If you take the time to find out a little bit about what these sociable customers have done, and then find a way to bring it up in conversation, you will have made a friend for life.

4. Emphasize the cutting edge. Tell them that your product will make them a leader, or allow them to use the best of innovation.

5. Emphasize the future. Tell them that while other companies settle for the status quo, you are sure they would be interested in moving into the future, because of their demonstrated leadership.

6. Get them to talk about themselves. Your conversational goal should be to present just a little information about yourself, and your own interests, in order to help them bond with you. After you have done this, stop talking about yourself and let them talk about themselves!

7. Use testimonials when appropriate and don't be afraid to drop names. While other people might dislike name droppers, sociable people don't. They want to know that you are plugged in.

8. Create a warm and friendly environment for the sale. Beware the sterile environment when you are trying to sell to the influential person. Get yourself out to a nice well-lit restaurant where there's the smell of fresh bread and the sound of people laughing.

9. Find out what their dreams are and encourage them. This rule applies to all people, as far as I know, but especially to influential/sociable people. Although I try to make my seminars as fun and upbeat as I can, while continuously searching for ways to encourage and praise the individual members of my audience, I am often saddened by the constant comments from people "that nobody really takes my dreams that seriously. They think my dreams are silly." I can't tell you how many people approach me after my seminars to thank me for encouraging their dreams.

It bothers me greatly when I hear comments like that, and then realize how many creative, fun, and talented people in this world probably give up because so many people who are close to them have a tendency to scoff or deride or roll their eyes at dreams or cherished ideas. So, if you want to be more successful with other people, especially your customers, make it a point to follow these rules and, especially, to find out what their dreams and ambitions are and show them that you believe in them, no matter what type they are. If you do this regularly, you will find that your circle of friends and customers will steadily increase.

Stress Points for the High I

Although stress has some of the same effects on everyone—creating anxiety, tension, and irritability, among other problems—it is important to know that when highly influential/sociable people are under stress, as they will readily admit, they often become depressed, unmotivated, and lethargic—especially when they think they are not fully appreciated or feel that people don't like them enough. But there is an antidote! It's called empathy.

Think of a human plant that needs to be watered four times a day with approval and friendship and you know what makes the predominantly *influential* person tick. If a high I becomes stressed at work, it is usually not because they have too much work to do. It is probably because they think they are doing a lot of work that no one appreciates. Therefore, the way to the highly sociable person's heart is affection, warmth, laughter, praise, encouragement, and friendship. Providing these will help you *help them* manage their stress! Also, with the highly influential/sociable person, it's okay to come right out and make jokes about how stressful life is when you're not appreciated. The high I will respond immediately to such statements and will not be offended.

Closing Strategies for the High I

- Be enthusiastic about the product. If you feel a friendship/kinship has been established, don't be afraid to try to close on the first call.

- Explain how the customer can improve his or her image through making the best buying decision quickly, and how this decision will help lead the company into the future.

- Give a range of alternatives from low cost to high cost. Sociable people seem to prefer the word "alternative" to "option." Driven people like the word "option" because it sounds businesslike and legal—the reason that sociable people do not. They like the word "alternative" because it sounds rich and rewarding—as in "a world full of possibilities and exciting alternatives in a universe full of interesting people to talk to and wonderful things to see." You get the picture.

- Be prepared for questions about benefits and incentives when an I is considering buying your product. Don't be surprised if the person asks if a free trip to the Bahamas is included.

- Always be prepared to explain what other leading companies are using your product.

- Make sure you say that you hope this purchase will be the beginning of a lifelong friendship or relationship.

- And finally, don't overlook the value of a thank-you card or note, whether or not you close. Build the relationship and it will pay off. Personally, I do not understand why more people do not send thank-you cards. I keep a stack of them on my desk ready to fill out and mail whenever I get the chance.

Before we move on to the rules of selling to the other two types of people in the world, I want to present you with a short intermediary chapter with strategies for dealing with anxiety.

CHAPTER 7

How to Protect Yourself from Guilt and Anxiety

Almost every human being, especially psychologists, can point to one idea that represents the most important thing they know. Sigmund Freud, for example, might have summed up his entire theory of mankind's woes with the idea that human beings are part animal instinct and part aspiring-angelic-perfectionist-hero-saint, and that the conflict between these two sides of us ultimately drives us nuts in the end.

The most important thing I know is this: There is a great human tendency to feel that everything anyone else feels is our own fault. This causes problems in how we feel about ourselves and how we market ourselves to others. People don't trust other people who have guilty looks on their faces. I wish I could walk around holding up a billboard in front of every human being who wants to feel happier and be a better salesperson, too.

What Other People Feel Is Not Your Fault!

Psychologists call the tendency to think that other peoples' problems and feelings are your fault "automatic thinking." As long as we closely adhere to our Marketing Identity Worksheet and our Sales Strategy Worksheet, and as long as we try our best not to be rude or say mean things to people, we should never have to feel that other peoples' worries and insecurities have anything to do with us.

I always try to convince all of my seminar participants to believe that the looks of worry and concern they often see on their customers' faces have nothing whatsoever to do with them. As a salesperson, it is critical to remember this if you want to be successful and stay sane. Remember, life is tough. Life is stressful. People have bad days and bounce checks. But do not, for one second, get in the habit of thinking other people have looks of concern and worry because they do not like you. This kind of automatic thinking will make you feel and look guilty. And as soon as you feel guilty, you will project guilt. That's bad.

Human beings can "smell" the feeling of guilt on others, and no one buys anything from people who look or "smell" guilty. Therefore, you must always force yourself to assume, no matter what the customer says or how he acts, that his problems are caused by something else. Instead, project helpfulness and control. By doing this, you will accomplish two important sales goals:

1. You will project yourself as a rescuer whose services are necessary.

2. You will help your troubled customer lose his own level of anxiety.

I simply cannot overemphasize the importance of the second point. It represents the most important secret of salesmanship. We live in a world of great anxiety. Everyone wants to feel a sense of peace. If you help people relieve their anxiety, they will feel indebted to you and will literally do anything for you. Your customers want your help getting back on the board of their own self-marketing plan. Tap into this concept and you will achieve more success than you ever imagined in your wildest dreams.

The Real Secret of Anxiety: Depression and Confusion

I want to make it extremely clear that, in this chapter, I am not talking about the kind of biologically or psychologically rooted chronic or short-term anxiety that is severe enough to warrant the help of a physician. I am talking about the kind of ordinary, garden-variety anxiety that almost all of us suffer from time to time when our personal, spiritual, and professional goals are in a state of confusion or conflict.

Of course there are instances in which some of us, because of our individual biology or exposure to overwhelmingly stressful circumstances, or both, will sometimes feel that we are trapped in a state of anxiety from which there is no escape, and we may suffer a combination of very painful physical and emotional and psychological symptoms at the same time. For example, some of us might feel a persistent sense of worry or impending doom, or constriction in the chest, or chest pain, or shortness of breath, or chronic insomnia, or stomach pains, or anything under the sun. There have been times in my life when I foolishly put myself under way too much stress and developed health problems because of it, including clinical anxiety. I am glad that in those moments I was smart enough to seek out the care of physicians who are specially trained to handle stress-related illness.

But this chapter isn't about the kind of anxiety that should lead you to commit yourself. It's about the kind of anxiety that you can avoid by learning how to stay focused and stop creating conflicts for yourself by trying to live the life others would have you lead, instead of living the life you want.

Are You Living Someone Else's Dream or Your Own?

As far as I can tell, a great deal of human anxiety, confusion, and depression is caused by simple things. This is especially true for highly stressed people in the business world because, like it or not, life is like a chess game. You start off on one side of the board with your mission in life, your values, and your strategy—all of the things you must fill in carefully on your Marketing Identity Worksheet. On the opposite side are the goals you want to accomplish in your life. The enemy represents all of those people who scoff at your dreams or want to see you fail. You want to checkmate these people by sticking to your mission and values and self-marketing strategy. As a matter of fact, if you always stick to these things, you will always win, eventually. Checkmate is virtually assured one day.

But you must stay on the board. You must stick to your plan. If you spend your time drinking or doing drugs, you have left the board. If you spend your time wallowing in hatred or anger or self-pity or thoughts of revenge, you have left the board. If you find yourself associating with people who are negative and destructive in their thinking, instead of positive and optimistic, you will soon leave the board. And the farther away you get from the board, the less chance you have of winning. And the more time you spend away from the board, the greater chance you have of losing it all, and the more anxiety, depression, and confusion you will feel because, inside your heart of hearts, you will know that you are letting yourself down.

As you have imagined by now, success is truly a "mind game"— and we must all remember, every single second of our lives, that the only mind we can ever really count on is our own. Therefore, if you come into contact with or try to form a relationship with any human beings who have a constant look of *anxiety, concern,* or *depression* on their faces, more often than not they are lost and separated from their own self-marketing plan.

These people want and need your help. They might not say it, but they do.

They want to be happy and focused again and to get back on the track of their dreams again.

They want to get back on the board, but they don't know how.

Now, how can you help them?

You can help them by trying to *visualize* where they are on the board. Then you try to find a way to explain to them how your product or service and their relationship with you will help them get back on the board! This is what the chessboard of life looks like.

The only way to really achieve maximum success in life is to get

Ye Olde Chess Game of Life

The Enemy Side

Scoffers
Hypocrites
People Who Laugh at Your Dreams
Jealous People
People Who Want to See You Fail

LAND OF ANXIETY
(Abbreviated List of Symptoms)

LAND OF CONFUSION
(Abbreviated List of Symptoms)

The Opposition

	Drugs	Hatred
	Alcohol	Envy
	Hypocrisy	Self-Pity
	Mean-spiritedness	Irresponsibility
	Vengefulness	Ungratefulness

Your Side

Your Mission
Your Values
Your Self-Marketing Strategy
"Your Plan"
Remember: Do Not Leave the Board!

from one side of the board to the other as quickly as possible, preferably in a straight line. If you or any of your potential customers is anywhere outside of the board, you're wasting time and you know it. The knowledge and realization that we are wasting time, when we know we are mortal and only have so many years to live before we die, taps into and aggravates our deepest and most primal fear—the fear of death. But when we are on the board—and maximizing our time and our potential for success—we know that, too. And that makes us feel, from a psychological standpoint, that we are achieving a measure of victory over death and beating the Grim Reaper at his own game.

Now, if you can convince your customers that you are *adding years to their lives* and can help them get back on the board and stop wasting time, thus helping them conquer their most primal fears and helping them relieve their levels of anxiety and depression, what chance do you think you have of building a long-term, profit-building relationship with these customers?

CHAPTER 8

Discerning People

I n this part of the book, we will look at how to sell to the discerning customer.

Although people who are primarily discerning might have dynamic traits, it is their discerning side that rules their behavior and mentality in the business world. I cannot overemphasize this for sales and marketing people.

The key word that defines the discerning customer is "careful."

Discerning people are careful people. They care about certain things a little more than dynamic customers. They care about accuracy. They care about details. They care about dotting "i"s and crossing "t"s. They care about the truth, the whole truth, and nothing but the truth. They care about credentials. They care about being careful.

Therefore, the discerning customer is a slow buyer and a cautious buyer. He also tends to be suspicious of strangers. As far as salespeople go, you are guilty until proven innocent.

Above all, you must always remember:

You Cannot Use a Dynamic Sales Approach on a Discerning Customer

You check your enthusiasm at the door. Do not appear flashy. Do not talk too fast. Do not be too chatty—and no jokes. You must move and talk very slowly and you must project carefulness. A completely different set of rules applies when your buyer is discerning and not dynamic.

Discerning customers are either highly conscientious (C) or highly steadfast (S). They are extremely methodical, careful, observant, and scrutinizing. If you feel like you are under a microscope in their presence, you are, so be prepared for a microscopic examination. These people need facts, figures, proof, and assurance of your professional expertise.

They are the hard sell.

Be ready.

Also be aware of the fact that *most* corporate buyers are discerning buyers. Think about it. If you are a CEO and your goal is to protect your company's assets, whom do you think you would put between the nation's salespeople and your company's bank account? A frantic driven person, an emotional sociable person, or a suspicious-minded, slow-moving, carefully methodical discerning person?

We are going to jump out of order and look at the conscientious person before the steadfast person for a pretty good reason. Most buyers and accountant types (your corporate money handlers) fall into the conscientious category, because they are the most suspicious, critical, judgmental, analyzing, dissatisfied, and nitpicky human beings ever born. And their employers know it. That's why they were hired.

But that's okay. I wouldn't want anyone else watching over my money, would you?

Because conscientious buyers are such a hard sell, it just makes more sense to talk about them first. That is to say, once you learn how to sell to conscientious customers, it will be easier to figure out how to best impress their more soft-spoken and less judgmental psychological cousins, abundantly sincere steadfast customers.

So let's turn the page now and enter the world of aloofness, criticism, suspiciousness, self-righteousness, and perpetual dissatisfaction—you know, the "real" world of sales.

CHAPTER 9

How to Sell to a Conscientious Person

While it might seem, from the comments I made in the preceding chapter, that it would be almost impossible to win a conscientious person over, it isn't. You just have to know how she thinks and operates.

And besides, I was intentionally being a little hyperbolic at the end of the last chapter when I described conscientious people as being critical, nitpicky people. I simply wanted to warn you about the conscientious person at his or her worst. Because when conscientious buyers are under stress, they indeed can act that way. More often than not, there's a good reason for it.

Think about the things other human beings do that aggravate you the most. Don't you sometimes feel that the world is full of idiots, bozos, and nincompoops? All of us feel that way from time to time, even if conscientiousness is not our primary trait. Conscientious people just have a lower threshold of patience for nincompoopery.

Let's take a look at the mindset of a few clear-cut conscientious people I know. For our first example, consider one of my good friends, Rena Kearney, who is by profession a podiatric medical assistant. Rena is one of the most naturally intelligent and capable people I have ever met. Not only is she called upon quite often to assist during foot surgery, she is also the first person anyone calls when any kind of machine breaks down. She has a higher mechanical aptitude than almost anyone I know, including most mechanics.

There is a machine in Rena's office called an autoclave that sterilizes medical instruments. Not too long ago, this machine broke down during the middle of the day. Rena got out her toolbox and took the machine apart. She reached inside the machine and pulled out a handful of tubes. After a few seconds she had deduced that one of the tubes was not receiving enough vacuum pressure. A few seconds later she had figured out why. Soon she had fixed the machine and it was up and running again.

While I was writing this chapter, I asked Rena to give me a short list of the things that aggravate her the most, in terms of people who are not like her. This is what she said: "I guess I don't understand why some people act differently. For example, why can't some people get out of bed in the morning and do what they're supposed to do? How can somebody lie in bed and not go look for a job if they know they have a bill to pay?

"Or how can some people stare at a stack of paperwork on their desk and not do something about it? It can face them all day long, and yet, they stare right past it as if it isn't even there, as if they don't even care. How can that be?

"Or you see someone speeding down the road a hundred miles an hour. Don't they realize that they could kill someone? Don't they see a connection? Don't they understand? Is it because they don't get it, or because they just don't care? And if they don't get it, how could they be so stupid? And if it's because they don't care, how could they not care? I don't understand."

Rena admits that her principal weakness is a slight tendency toward being judgmental, yet she says she is working on this "weakness" every day—or at least trying to.

"Sometimes we all have a tendency to make snap judgments about people," she said. "That's not wise, because we never really know what any person has been through, or where they're coming from, or what their own problems or difficulties might be. I make snap judgments myself sometimes, although I am trying to correct that tendency in myself. Because when you really get down to it, we are essentially ignorant of what other people have been through, and it's ignorance that gets us into trouble with other people—and ourselves—every time. Not stupidity but ignorance. Stupidity means you're mentally deficient, but ignorance, which is a different concept, means that you haven't taken the time to learn. Ignorance is worse, if you ask me."

These observations by Rena Kearney represent a succinct description of the "conscientious" mindset. Yet, there is one final component of the mindset that is extremely important to bear in mind—and I would describe it as the ultimate "fly in the ointment" of life, insofar as the way conscientious people view the world.

The central grievance conscientious people seem to have with others is well described by another friend of mind, Lenee Woods. Lenee is also possessed of an inordinate amount of natural intelligence and thus has that built-in "eye-rolling" tendency that all Cs have when they contemplate the shortcomings of others less diligent than they.

"It's not ignorance or stupidity that bothers me," Lenee says. "What bothers me, down in the pit of my soul, is willful ignorance. When you have the information available but you choose not to use it. When you choose not to learn. That profoundly bothers me. I just don't see any excuse for that. I think willful ignorance is wrong."

This very same attitude and mindset is shared by most highly conscientious people, many of whom work as accountants, lawyers, surgeons, police officers, or, for our purposes, corporate buyers. As marketing experts in this chapter will testify, most corporate buyers are Cs. And as the experts will also testify, most corporate buyers, no matter what their title or experience might be, ultimately view the world the same way Rena and Lenee do.

So, in any major business sales meeting, this is the kind of mindset you are up against.

Another piece of information you need to digest is this: Most conscientious people, although they are extremely critical, are actually a lot more humble than you would think. For example, most celebrated doctors and scientists I have met are highly conscientious people, but far from the stereotype. Most of these distinguished doctors and scientists are actually very humble, believe it or not—and I am talking about those people who are generally accepted to be the best in their field. They might be somewhat impatient with the rest of humanity, on occasion, but that does not mean they aren't humble. Perhaps you have noticed yourself that those people who are acknowledged to be the best in their field are usually quiet and unpretentious. It's always those second-class professionals or wannabes who are arrogant and obnoxious because they are fundamentally insecure.

Being humble means that you realize that at any given second you could make a terrible mistake. Making mistakes is not an option, though, when you have a drill bit inside someone's head. Think for a moment about how doctors are trained. In undergraduate studies, one of the courses they have to master is organic chemistry, a course that features the most aggravating laboratory requirements ever devised. Most organic chemistry experiments take about six hours to complete—not including the paperwork, which takes another couple of hours. During these experiments, you have to stare at a little flask waiting for things to drip. If you mess up anywhere along the line, and you don't get the right kind of drip, you have to start all over. So it's not unreasonable to expect that you might spend twelve hours on one experiment that is only part of one class out of five others you have to take each semester that are just as demanding.

Some people in less demanding majors might not even spend twelve hours studying during the entire semester for all of their courses combined.

So it's easy to see, after finishing twelve years of such schooling, how doctors might be a little on the cranky side. But they have been turned into scientists and for the most part have become extraordinarily careful. They have been taught to realize that at any given second, they could be wrong—and being wrong is not an option. No matter how you slice it, that is the mindset of humility. Only arrogant people consider that they could never be wrong.

On the advisory board of Industrial Footcare, we are fortunate enough to have the participation of a brilliant neurosurgeon, Robert

Lacin, M.D. Dr. Lacin has a medical degree from Switzerland, has fought in the Israeli Army, and is an assistant professor of neurosurgery at Duke University Medical Center. He is also one of the most modest, humble, soft-spoken, friendly, and unpretentious human beings I have ever met.

Now this is a person I have seen go into someone's back with a scalpel, open up the body down to the spinal column, expose the spinal column, locate a damaged section of bone, remove the bone from around the spinal cord, fashion a new section of spinal column out of a wedge of leg bone, put the new bone he just carved into the gap in the spinal column, tap it down with a miniature hammer, inspect for defects in his work, give the thumbs-up sign that all is well, and then sew the patient back up and prepare him to go home in less than half an hour.

His comments after all this? "No big deal. Who's next?"

This hallmark attitude of extreme carefulness and humility characterizes almost every genuinely capable and many of the supersuccessful people I have met.

In the worlds of business and marketing, as well as in the worlds of science and medicine, it is imperative to realize that most of the people *really* running the show seem to be careful and humble types. Look around. If you run across a person who appears wildly arrogant, pompous, and rude, simply shrug him off and keep looking for the "real boss." More than likely that pompous person you just met is not really in charge. That's why he is pompous and rude.

But, when you do find the *real* decision maker, don't expect the process to be easy. Even if most real decision makers are humble, they're also demanding. If such people even get a whiff of an impression that you are not also careful and humble, you will get on their bad side.

With that thought in mind, let us dissect the mentality of conscientious people even further so that we will effectively learn how to make no mistakes when trying to work with them and get on their level of carefulness.

Chief Characteristics of the Conscientious Person

As we have suggested already, the primary traits of conscientious people are the following:

- They are conservative.

- They are controlled, especially with their thoughts and emotions.

- They are cautious and suspicious of strangers: You are guilty until proven innocent.

- They are obsessive about quality, accuracy, and details.

- They expect you to care about the same things they care about.

What Motivates the Conscientious, Long-Term Buyer?

From a sales standpoint, you are trying to motivate the conscientious person to feel safe, to trust you, and to believe and know that you are going to be very careful with the needs analysis you help to investigate before selling her a new product. In other words, you are trying to motivate her to buy.

You are not, I repeat *not*, turning up the volume on the level of excitement or enthusiasm in the sales meeting. That is the opposite of what you want to do. You can only motivate the conscientious person to buy by toning down your level of enthusiasm so that you create the feeling that everything is proceeding in a calm, controlled, careful, and orderly fashion.

In other words, conscientious people want you to look, feel, sound, and smell ethical.

Ethical—now there's an important and popular word. But what does it really mean? During the time I have been writing this book, there has been increased media attention on the subject of ethics in sales, and a great deal of speculation as to what causes an atmosphere of loose ethics inside any organization. In the December 1997 edition of *Sales & Marketing Management*, I read a very thorough and interesting report on the issue of ethics. The author, Michele Marchetti, began the report by citing some depressing statistics, including the observations that 49 percent of sales managers say they have heard sales reps lie on the job, and that 54 percent of sales managers say that the drive to meet sales goals does a disservice to customers.

Then the report introduced a list of companies that have become embroiled in controversies regarding ethics in sales—which raises a fairly self-evident point: If corporate leadership promotes or allows unethical behavior, why in the world would anyone expect individual sales reps on the street to act any differently? The issue few people seem to be addressing is this: Corporate leadership that does not teach ethical, careful, and methodical salesmanship on the street level is unbelievably shortsighted and self-destructive.

Read the following quote carefully: "According to sales professionals and experts, the driving force behind this questionable activity [unethical sales behavior] is the pressure to do business in today's combative marketplace. The stress brought on by quotas, pay plans, and a selling environment that encourages fierce competition is, in too many cases, eroding morality."

Yes, Ms. Marchetti is right. The kind of pressure to sell at any cost is helping to erode morality. But is such pressure smart, in the long run? No, it's shortsighted—and the salesmanship and business equivalent of strip mining or clear-cutting.

The pressure to meet sales quotas at any cost causes many companies to eventually sour relationships with potential long-term buyers. Unfortunately, the mentality that drives an "immediate earnings gratification" style of selling ignores the long-term fertility of the money garden. It's what I call killing the golden goose.

Look at it this way: Every conscientious buyer you come into contact with—even all of your current and potential buyers combined—represents the goose that lays the golden eggs, or in other words, your dependable yearly sales, month after month, year after year.

This buying goose, on average, is a careful goose. She's a conscientious goose. She's moral, ethical, cautious, and slow to make buying decisions. She was handpicked by top executives who intentionally placed a careful buyer between you (the salespeople of the world) and the company's bank account.

If you want to make money for a long time with this buying goose, you have to be nice to her. You can't lie. You can't try to coerce her into buying things she doesn't need. You can't manipulate facts, because if you lie or exaggerate, chances are she'll catch you. Oftentimes, she'll catch you the very first time you lie, and if she doesn't catch you the first time, she'll certainly catch you the second. And then she'll never speak to you again.

When companies put inordinate pressure on their salespeople, this, in effect, is what they are saying: "Bob, Sally, I want you to walk into that office across the street, find the goose, shoot the goose, skin it, cook it, and give it back to our stockholders. Now! Do it! Our stockholders are hungry! They gotta eat! And they love to eat golden goosemeat! So go! Go, go, go!"

If you want to devote three or four years of your life working for a company that thinks like that, go ahead. But no matter how hard you work for this company, you're going to get fired eventually, because there will be no more geese left to kill.

Now this conundrum, of course, raises a few interesting dilemmas. If you are a businessperson, the dilemma of trying to meet sales quotas while building trust with the long-term buyer puts you right smack dab between a rock and a hard place. How do you get out of this dilemma? You can't. If you're in business, you're stuck. There's no way out. You will always be there. However, there are certain maneuvers you can make that will allow you to maintain your sanity.

How to Steer Your Boat When You're Caught between Scylla and Charybdis

Like all great mythological heroes, great businesspeople must know what to do when confronted with sea monsters that turn into rocks, or when trying to navigate around teeming whirlpools and other distracting nuisances that crop up from time to time. The best advice I have heard so far with regard to navigating that rock and hard place—the need for fulfilling sales quotas while cultivating relationships with cautious buyers—comes from Timothy L. O'Connor, who, at the time of this writing, was a division sales manager for EBI Medical Systems.

According to Tim, using psychology is your only way out:

Many people are confused when it comes to selling to the conscientious, long-term, ethical buyer. As we all know, this is the most challenging customer for the average salesperson. Additionally, many companies today specifically recruit individuals with this personality type to stand between the salesperson and the corporation's money.

Therefore, the successful salesperson of the next century must learn to be a chameleon. He must effectively blend his needs and those of the company he represents with the needs of the customer. Thus, the modern salesperson serves the role of diplomat.

But this poses particular problems when coupled with the instant gratification expected by today's investors. The trickle-down effect of earnings expectations ultimately rests upon the shoulders of the salesperson. How the salesperson handles this pressure will determine his success.

For instance, the high C buyer cannot feel pressured to make decisions. However, a salesperson can reasonably push a high D toward a quicker decision. This is how one must develop a short- and long-term strategy to the selling process.

In light of these nuances, assessing customers and their personalities is more crucial today than at any other time. Because of that, I'm actually going to make this book required reading for all our salespeople.

Tim, along with other highly successful sales managers I have met, seems to comprehend, on a profound level, the need to hire ethical salespeople, in lieu of spending tons of money on "ethics training" programs. It's not as difficult as you might think, if you know what to look for.

How to Select Ethical Salespeople

Since there has been so much discussion in the press lately of the importance of ethical salesmanship, sales managers might well find themselves wondering how one goes about picking an ethical salesperson in the first place. Short of giving out some kind of psychology-based hiring questionnaire to help you hire salespeople, I think that what you are essentially looking for when you hire a salesperson is someone who is confident without being cocky. There's a huge difference.

> *Confident.* Does the person smile? Does he have energy? Does he have warmth? Does he show controlled enthusiasm? Is he well groomed? Is he proud of his accomplishments? Does he have a competitive streak? Is he polite?

> *Not Cocky.* Does she seem genuinely interested in what you have to say? Has she taken any notes? Has she responded to your comments with thoughtful responses? Does she talk about her past success in a levelheaded way, without bragging?

If you have received positive answers to these questions, and the candidate seems not to have lied, exaggerated, or falsified credentials, then chances are he or she will treat your customers the same way.

People who are confident without being cocky—unless they happen to be brilliant sociopaths who have learned to act that way for the sake of deception—generally have a strong character and a sense of ethics. And when you really get down to it, the ethics of any company are only as weak or as strong as the ethics of every single salesperson who represents that company out on the street. So if you are a sales director with hiring power, you have to realize that the ethical character and integrity of your company partly rests upon your decision-making shoulders.

Good salespeople, of course, need to have a strong, driven, competitive, conquering side, but they also have to know how to adopt the careful persona. That is because, more often than not, they will be trying to sell your company to overly careful customers. Therefore, they need to know what these overly careful customers like.

What Conscientious Customers Like

Cautious buyers like people who seem to be calm, careful, and organized in all things. Everything counts. They will notice whether or not your clothes match. They will check to see how organized your briefcase is. If you call from your car phone in a hysterical voice to say you are late, you have about as much of a chance of succeeding with them as the proverbial snowball.

Cautious buyers want to know that every person or product they are involved with will help improve accuracy, precision, and efficiency.

Cautious, conscientious buyers are suspicious of jokes. You must maintain an aura of strict business. Talk slowly and be careful. Let them see you taking notes. Ask careful questions about their needs and make an effort to carefully clarify your points of discussion. Make an effort to let them know you want to be very careful in assessing their needs.

Also, cautious customers like tried-and-true products. You will have to provide a lot of facts and figures to sell them cutting-edge products. We will analyze these traits in greater detail shortly, but first let us talk briefly about the issue of stress as it relates to the cautious buyer.

As important as knowing what conscientious buyers like is knowing what they don't like or what stresses them out. Here are some of the basics:

Stress Points for the High C

Cs under stress tend to show the following characteristics:

- They become very suspicious (they give you that raised eyebrow and fixed stony gaze).

- They become very distrustful.

- They display obsessive-compulsive behavior. Everything has to be in perfect order.

- They become overly controlling. The sacred status quo must be protected at all costs!

- They become extremely perfectionistic and exacting.

- They become extremely rigid and inflexible.

Exercise. Explore your own nitpicky side. In the spaces below, write down some of your own conscientious traits.

My conscientious characteristics:

1. _____

2. _____

3. _____

4. _____

5. _____

My stress points (what annoys me, aggravates me, or stresses me out):

1. _____

2. _____

3. _____

4. _____

5. _____

Now that you have given personal responses to the two categories above, let's give some thought to the most important question of all: What calms me down?

This question is of paramount importance when you are trying to put yourself into the mindset of conscientious/careful buyers. Your goal is to help calm them down, make them feel like you are diminishing the stress in their life, instead of adding to it, and that everything you do will proceed in a careful, orderly fashion.

Write down in the spaces below the kind of things other people can do to help calm you down when you are under stress or feeling pressured:

What calms me down:

1. _____

2. _____

3. _____

4. _____

5. _____

Let us now look at the key rules for selling to the conscientious/cautious buyer, keeping in mind that what motivates them and builds trust in them is also the same thing that calms them down.

How to Sell to the Conscientious/Cautious Buyer

- Be armed to the teeth with background information, facts, figures, and testimonials from reputable people.

- Give the customer time to digest details and facts before you proceed to the next step.

- Don't rush the customer or be too talkative! Act dignified and precise. Be prepared to answer all questions in a precise, scientific, orderly manner.

- Make sure all of your presentation materials are neat.

- Make sure your presentation speech is concise, logical, and orderly.

- Avoid the hard sell like the plague. Keep your voice even and calm, and measured.

- Show unwavering dedication to your own company and products, but don't come off as overly enthusiastic or showman-like.

- Recommend several meetings so that the customer can have ample time to evaluate the product and make a good decision.

- Emphasize that you want the customer to have the opportunity to examine and interpret the facts, and to draw his own conclusions.

- Emphasize any warranties or guarantees that minimize the customer's risk.

- Emphasize and reiterate that you stand behind your product 100 percent.

- Try to emphasize loss of time, productivity, money, or efficiency that may be caused by not buying your product, or by delaying the purchase.

- Do not make promises you can't keep, and make sure that the printed information in your sales package matches your verbal presentation.

Clarify, Clarify, Clarify, Clarify: The Four-Part Sales Meeting Rule

There is no word that conscientious/cautious buyers like to hear more than the word "clarify." It is simply impossible to use this word too many times in the presence of cautious buyers.

They want to hear it. They expect you to say it. If you do not say it they won't like you. The word "clarify" must come out of your mouth.

Also, there is nothing that a cautious buyer abhors more than a salesperson who gives the impression of wanting to close on the first meeting. That just doesn't look or sound careful. It will never happen. Plus, it is a strong indication that the salesperson has no interest in clarifying.

When selling the cautious corporate buyer, you simply have to get it through your head that it will take at least four meetings with the customer before you can close. These meetings include the first clarification meeting, at least two other reclarification meetings, and then a final ultraclarification and paper-signing meeting.

Below is a drill with the text and outline of your prototype "cautious buyer" sales approach. It will get straight to the point and save you some time.

Initial Call

Good morning, Mr./Ms. Conscientious Buyer. I am calling to follow up on the one-page letter I mailed to you last week, outlining the benefits of my product/service for your company. I also enclosed some data about its usefulness elsewhere and our track record of success. I am calling to see if we can set up an initial meeting, if you have a level of interest, in order to begin the process of clarifying your needs with regard to this product. I envision this as the first step in a careful analysis of your expectations and needs. But I believe such a careful analysis will help me provide you with some solid, useful cost-saving information.

Of course, you should use your own words, but a calm, level-headed approach like this will get you in the door. Once you are in the door, you will earn a tremendous amount of trust with the cautious buyer if you suggest a series of meetings before the buyer has a chance to suggest it. This will earn you major brownie points. Here is what will happen during these requisite four (or more) meetings:

Meeting 1. You come in with an initial succinct proposal that has been mailed to the buyer in advance. You bring an extra copy in case the buyer needs another. You say you want to review the proposal and begin the process of clarifying needs. The buyer makes some favorable comments on your proposal and then begins to talk. You keep your mouth shut and take a lot of notes. You don't try to sell yet, unless the buyer says she wants to purchase. When the buyer has finished talking, you say you want to go home, review your notes, send a revised proposal, and then come back next week at a convenient time to discuss the revisions, which you will mail beforehand. The buyer begins to like you. You've made it to first base.

Meeting 2. You mail in your revised proposal and then come back in. The buyer is happy to see you and has a few points that need to be readdressed. You take more notes and offer to go back to the drawing board one more time to polish your sales proposal. You shake hands and leave. Now the buyer really likes you. Now you're safely at second base.

Meeting 3. You have mailed in yet another proposal. You go back to see the buyer. This time the buyer has only a few additional thoughts or concerns, but you take copious notes and promise to research these concerns and revise your proposal once again. You shake hands and leave. You are on third base.

Meeting 4. You mail in your next revised proposal and the buyer calls to say she is very impressed. She has one small point she wants to reclarify but says you can bring the papers to the next meeting, because she is ready to sign. You show up and do the last reclarification. You are calm and relaxed. You talk a lot about long-term follow-up service and long-term relationships. Then you sign the $250,000 contract. You are very glad you were patient as you contemplate all the ways you can spend your money. Home run.

How to Ruin Your Relationship with the C

Do not get too personal with Cs unless you know them very well. Don't try to talk about friends or family, or social groups. They will feel you are being too familiar and will mistrust you. Stick to business.

Do not touch them. Don't touch them on the shoulder, or pat

them on the back. No physical contact whatsoever, except for a businesslike handshake—unless you want them to think you are a molester.

Avoid a loud, emotional sales presentation. Do not laugh or smile too much. Do not tell jokes. Be warm and friendly, but highly reserved.

Do not give shallow, pat answers to questions. Be factual and prepared.

Closing Strategies for the High C

Never attempt to close with a conscientious buyer on the first visit unless he makes it clear that he wants to buy. He just won't do it.

- Closing with a conscientious buyer is more of a process than an event. As the lengthy process unfolds, step by step, through all of the meetings we discussed above, be sure to thoroughly discuss your own qualifications and explain the background and reputation of your company.

- Carefully explain why your product is a proven product and explain all warranties and guarantees. Help the customer see how you will minimize his risk.

- Allow the customer to wait before closing, but get him to commit to a follow-up time. Be consistent, calm, and dependable with your follow-up.

- Allow the C customer, if possible, to use the product on a trial basis.

- Recommend that the C customer put down a deposit on the product while he is thinking about it.

These basic rules and strategies you use for a C customer are very much like those you'd use to sell the steadfast person, with a few twists.

We'll discuss these twists in the next chapter.

CHAPTER 10

How to Sell to a Steadfast Person

I like to tell everyone that everything I know about sales and marketing I learned while working as a bag boy at the Piggly Wiggly grocery store in La Grange, North Carolina, during my last year of high school. That summer I had several jobs including working in tobacco fields trying to save as much money as possible for my forthcoming tuition at the University of North Carolina at Chapel Hill, where I knew my entertainment expenses would also be high.

During that summer at the Piggly Wiggly, I was privileged to study under three great masters: Russell Bartlett, Jeffrey Lane, and an exceptional young salesman by the name of Ben Suggs. Ben Suggs's professional title was "stocking clerk," but he was also a superb salesman and marketing savant. Many of the principles that I have since seen displayed by top executives seemed to be automatic to Ben Suggs even at that early point in his life career.

Through the prism of time, I now realize that working at a Piggly Wiggly in eastern North Carolina represented the ultimate sales training incubator, since North Carolina seems to have more than its fair share of steadfast people. Steadfast people, as I will explain later on in this chapter, have predictable traits. They are extremely hardworking, fair, honest, reliable, trustworthy, community oriented,

121

family oriented, and patriotic. They also have high standards when it comes to customer service. They expect you to treat them with the same respect and honesty that you would give to members of your own family.

That is why I have chosen to introduce this chapter on selling to steadfast people with a reminiscence from my Piggly Wiggly days. Because over a period of many years, I have finally learned that the best customer service is steadfast service. Service that is geared toward steadfastness emanates from a philosophy of both salesmanship and customer care that requires you to treat your customers as your kin.

Granted, our young friend Ben was a real character, and everyone realized he was a character, even the customers. But the point is everyone knew that in spite of his occasional theatrics he took the art of salesmanship seriously, and he genuinely took his customers seriously as well. When you get right down to it, that's what steadfast customers want to see.

With that in mind, let me now explain why it was that Ben Suggs, the stocking clerk with a shiny gold tooth and an infectious smile, was able to teach us all so much about the art of customer service and sales.

Ben had an uncanny ability to understand the psychology and motivation of the customers who came into the Piggly Wiggly. In fact, as soon as any customer approached the checkout counter, Ben could tell you which car the person had arrived in, even if he had not seen the person arrive, simply by matching up the person's appearance—clothing style, hair, and the way the person carried himself or herself—with the selection of automobiles in the parking lot. I had never seen anything like it, and have not since.

Another thing that Ben seemed particularly good at was knowing which customers would be more likely to give him a tip, should he serve as their bag boy, and which would be more likely to give me a tip, based upon his innate knowledge of human psychology and personality types. He spent many hours explaining his philosophy to me. Ben's theory was that most customers like to tip those people they think truly understand them and their needs. He was also convinced that customers know immediately whether a bag boy or any other person understands them and knows where they're coming from, or whether the person serving them could care less about their needs. In other words, Ben Suggs, a teenager, already knew how to mind-read his customers. Since the rest of us weren't master sales-people yet, Ben Suggs tried to help us along.

Using his sophisticated and instinctual knowledge of human be-havior and human psychology, Ben helped us make bigger tips by diverting the flow of potential customers to the right bag boys. That is, he would survey the crowd of customers as they began to mill toward the checkout stand and would figure out which customer would be more likely to form a bonding relationship with which par-ticular bag boy. His sense of skill in this area was uncanny. When left to our own devices, we oftentimes found ourselves dealing with customers who did not seem to like us one bit and who seemed to have no interest in tipping us whatsoever. However, if we left the selection process up to Ben, we almost inevitably found ourselves dealing with customers who liked us and who felt that they were "on our level." We also found ourselves grinning as we came back from the parking lot time after time, our pockets bulging with tips.

In this way, Ben Suggs endeared himself to everyone and proved to be a great financial boon to us bag boys. I must point out, how-ever, that the benefit of studying under Ben Suggs did not come with-out a price. The downside was that all of us lived with the constant threat of knowing that at any given moment, if we weren't properly attending to our customers' needs, Suggs might intervene on the customer's behalf and criticize our technique in front of the entire store.

Ben used this strategy to his own advantage on many occasions to impress his own customers and to create an even higher tipping situation for himself. For example, if, by accident, I were to get a hold of one of Ben's preferred customers before Ben had a chance to di-vert the flow of customers according to his own precise methodol-ogy, he would keep a careful eye on me the entire time I was bagging the customer's groceries. If he saw me making the slightest deviation in the standard bagging techniques the customer preferred, he would immediately leave his own station and come to mine, instructing me in the ways to improve my relationship with the customer. For example, he might interrupt me and say: "Stop! Don't you realize that Mrs. Smith likes to have all of her bread in one bag? And that she likes to have all of her frozen foods in another bag? Don't you know? Haven't you served Mrs. Smith enough times to know that? Don't you *care*? Don't you care enough to want to bag her groceries the way she wants them bagged?" And so on. These types of comments, inevitably, would provoke laughter from the other bag boys. It was just a part of Ben's personality that we all had to accept. The good side of the experience, of course, is that we all learned a lot about customer service from Ben. And make no mistake about it, after Ben had interrupted a bagging procedure and had taken matters into his own hands, you could be virtually assured that he would come back from the parking lot with an astronomical tip in his pocket. So it was obvious that he knew what he was doing, that he knew what he was talking about, and that he was a person well worth observing in the workplace. Therefore, when I tell people that almost everything I know about customer service, sales, and marketing I learned at the Piggly Wiggly as a bag boy, I'm not kidding.

To the discerning reader, it might seem that Ben's theatrics would make a truly steadfast person uncomfortable. But his sense of humor, his aura of genuine concern for the customer, and his infectious gold-toothed grin were his trump cards. Watching him at work, you would see weather-beaten steadfast farmers who looked like they hadn't smiled in forty years struggle in vain to keep themselves from smiling ear to ear, and slowly nodding with approval. You could tell that they appreciated both the entertainment and the message. Sales without an entertainment factor is boring to anyone. But the message must always be the same. The customer is boss. I don't know who taught Ben the secret, but he had the formula down pat.

Take a careful look at the techniques that Ben Suggs was using innately at that age.

1. He already knew that it is paramount to understand the individual psychology of the customer.

2. He understood the utmost importance of making customers feel that you are exactly the same kind of person that they are.

3. He understood that most customers only like to give their money to people they think are just like them.

4. He understood on a deep and implicit level that the more times you tell the customer how much you care and the more dramatically you emphasize this point, the more money you will make.

If I were forced to give the four top rules of salesmanship as I know it, it would be those. And Ben Suggs already knew them way back when, when we were all working at the Piggly Wiggly.

Additional Rules for Selling to the Steadfast Person

This chapter deals with rules and strategies for selling to the steadfast customer. Steadfast customers, as we have discussed elsewhere, are the psychological cousins of the conscientious type, since they fall into the group of people I call "discerning."

The difference between the predominantly steadfast person and the predominantly conscientious person, however, is critical—the steadfast person, according to my own experience, is a behavioral type characterized by an essentially nonjudgmental attitude toward other people. But this does not mean that the steadfast behavioral type does not have pet peeves of his or her own.

Like the conscientious person, the steadfast person tends to move a lot slower and appear less agitated than the dynamic person, who is characterized by a state of near constant high energy.

But just because the steadfast person or conscientious person tends to move more slowly and carefully, you cannot assume for one second that his or her mental processes are slower. In many cases, I find steadfast people have a more profound and discerning grasp of people and events than any other type I know.

According to some studies, steadfast people may comprise up to 40 percent of the U.S. population. I think the important point is this: A lot of your customers, especially your grassroots customers, are of the steadfast behavioral type. And unlike their conscientious cousins, steadfast people tend to be much more forgiving of others' faults, more tolerant, and more compassionate—but that does not mean they do not have their own high standards.

In a nutshell, steadfast people are extremely patriotic and moral. And although they may be forgiving of people's lapses in morality or steadfastness, they are not prone to develop relationships with businesspeople who do not have a high code of ethics and morality. So, if you want to be forgiven by a steadfast person, no matter what you do, you can virtually count on it. But if you want to develop a business relationship with a steadfast person, cultivate a high code of honor, morality, ethics, standards, and patriotism.

From a psychological point of view, I like to call the steadfast person the "Mount Everest mountain climber," meaning the steadfast person is extremely diligent and methodical and, as the name suggests, incredibly reliable and steady in their efforts. If the steadfast person tells you that she plans to get to the top of Mount Everest, she will get to the top of Mount Everest somehow, some way, no matter how long it takes, even if she loses both hands and feet to frostbite during the climb. She will continue climbing the mountain, even if she has to chew her way to the top. Steadfast people simply cannot be stopped. When they are under stress, however, their tendency is to become extremely slow and stubborn. At times of high stress, they may move so slowly you will find it difficult to tell if they're still alive. But they are still moving and they will not be stopped.

From an ego point of view, these kinds of people are virtually indestructible. Because of their high code of honor, their nonjudgmental attitude toward other human beings, their severe work ethic, their dependability, and their friendliness, I think the best description of the steadfast person is the salt of the earth type. That is, when people are speaking of the so-called salt of the earth, I think they are really talking about your steadfast behavioral-type person.

When I was growing up, my mother always told me that she considered people in eastern North Carolina to be the salt of the earth. It's funny, but recent experiences in the workplace have suggested that she might be right, even from a scientific, statistical point of view.

Not too long ago, I was invited to conduct a business seminar for a large group of people in eastern North Carolina, which included a majority of the workforce from the local telephone company. As I always do, I requested that the seminar participants take the DISC inventory as a prerequisite for the seminar.

When the test had been completed and the scores were computed, I asked to see a show of hands among the different behavioral types. I wanted to know how many driven people were in the room, how many influential people, how many conscientious people, and how many steadfast people. First, I turned to the employees from the large telephone company and asked to see a show of hands from those who had scored highest for the driven characteristic. No one raised a hand. Then I asked to see how many people were in attendance from that company. Again, no one raised a hand. The same thing for conscientious people. No one in the company had scored highest for the conscientious trait on their DISC inventory. Then I asked, perhaps without needing to, how many steadfast people were in the crowd. And everyone raised their hands. Of course, we all laughed. Interestingly, most of the other people in attendance from other companies were also predominantly of the steadfast trait.

Now I don't know if this is just a phenomenon that is particular to eastern North Carolina, but I got the distinct impression that there are a lot of steadfast-type people living out there in neighborhoods around me. And I have a hunch that the same phenomenon exists across the heartland of America, based upon the results of studies I have read.

This is important to know from a sales perspective because the steadfast consumer has a distinct personality and has distinct gripes and pet peeves when coming into contact with the business world. Some of the basics should be obvious:

- Steadfast people recoil at the sight of slick salesmen.

- Steadfast people recoil when they get even the slightest whiff that someone is dishonest or deceitful in any way.

- Steadfast people recoil when they get the slightest impression that a company is fly-by-night and does not have a longstanding reputation of excellence and steadfast qualities with its own customers.

- Steadfast people have an almost vehement intolerance for those who do not mean what they say and say what they mean.

Profile of the Steadfast/Sincere Person

Traits.   Very loyal and steadfast. Will stick to a project until it gets done, no matter how long it takes. Methodical mountain climbers. You can count on them to get to the top of Mount Everest—one step at a time. Patient. They enjoy a good team environment. Believe in giving service for a long time. Very traditional. Have high family values and a strict moral code.

Motivations.   Steadfast people like others who display a high sense of family and moral values, and a strict code of integrity. They are wary of the "slick deal" and would rather give five dollars to a hardworking, honest person than fifty cents to a shifty-eyed showman, even if they're selling the same thing.

High S people value actions over words. Show them you are dependable and keep your empty words to a minimum. Make sure that you present yourself as patriotic and industrious. Do not make hollow promises. And do not offer slick, dubious testimonials. These are the kind of people who literally gag when people show false or syrupy emotion. They don't mix well with promotional people and they tend to associate with their own type.

Stress Points for the High S

Ss under stress tend to show the following characteristics:

- They become very sluggish and apathetic.

- They move very slowly, and become like a turtle with its head in its shell.

- They become extremely unexpressive and nonemotional. They totally shut down.

- They become extremely inflexible, possessive, and territorial.

- They develop grudges that stick like peanut butter to the roof of your mouth.

Exercise.   In the spaces below, write down some of the other behavioral characteristics and stress points of some people you know—either friends, family members, acquaintances, or customers—who clearly fit the steadfast pattern of behavior. (You might even be describing yourself.)

Characteristics I have observed in steadfast people:

1. _____

2. _____

3. _____

4. _____

5. _____

Stress points I have noticed in steadfast people:

1. _____

2. _____

3. _____

4. _____

5. _____

With these thoughts in mind, let us consider the basic techniques for building rapport with the steadfast behavioral type.

Techniques for Doing Business with the Steadfast Person

Profile.   Loyal, dependable, good listener, patient, composed, relaxed, hard to ruffle, consistent

Demographics.   About 40 percent of the U.S. population

How to Sell to the Steadfast Person

- S is slow to make changes, so be patient.

- Develop a sense of trust. Show integrity and a work ethic.

- Demonstrate that you are loyal to your business, your promises, your products, and your customers.

- Don't push innovative or unproven products. Stick with traditional approaches.

- Any time you can make a link to family or team stability, do it.

- Provide lots of proof, statistics, and recommendations from steadfast sources, such as *Consumer Reports.*

- Answer all questions in a methodical, low-key, matter-of-fact way.

- Avoid any impression of being an arrogant blowhard.

- Make it clear that you have no problem making repeat visits.

- Ask plenty of questions so the customer knows you want to provide a perfect match between his or her needs and your services and products.

- Offer a list of satisfied customers he or she can call.

- Offer an action plan for studying the purchase before the final sale. Offer a trial period.

- Involve the family or work team in the buying decision whenever possible.

- Show sincerity!

Building Rapport with the High Steadfast Customer

The basic rule for doing business with steadfast people is to try to emphasize the added security or safety that will result from their timely purchase. Help them to feel a sense of assurance and low risk about their decision. Don't pressure. Give full explanations. Demonstrate that your program or product will do a complete job, so they won't have to make an additional purchase.

Also, be prepared to discuss your track record. Remember, these people will be watching you closely. They don't often buy from strangers; they are more likely to buy from neighbors, people who have earned their trust over the years.

In eastern North Carolina, many people talk about the three-year rule. If you move into a town anywhere in eastern North Carolina and you set up shop as a salesperson, you had better bring enough money along to tide you over for three years, or have another job, because during those three years people will be closely examining you to see if you have the following traits:

- Are you dependable? Is your word your bond?

- Are you community-oriented? (Do you give to the community or help out with things like Cub Scouts and Little League?) Do you honor God and country?

- Do you have a sense of responsibility and duty?

- Are you good to your family?

- Are you loyal to your friends?

- Do you pay your bills?

- Are you genuine? Do you walk as you talk and try not to be something you're not?

If, for some reason, you fall short of these traits during the three-year inspection and approval process, you might as well pack up and go back to where you came from because no one is going to buy anything from you. But if you pass, you will be welcomed into the community and people will begin to buy from you. As a matter of fact, if they find you to be loyal, they will be much more inclined to buy your products or services than the products or services of a stranger, even if your products and services are slightly more expensive.

And even if you are not a door-to-door salesperson, but are trying to mass market to the steadfast type, it would probably be in your best interest to understand the psychological meaning of the preceding standards of behavior when you are analyzing the content and messages of your advertising or marketing campaigns.

How Not to Ruin Your Relationship with the Steadfast Person

The basic rule for not ruining your relationship with the steadfast person is this: Don't go too fast! Don't be overly friendly or "schmoozy."

Don't be pushy or talk about closure too soon. Allow repeat visits. And don't bad-mouth other products or suppliers.

It will make steadfast people dislike you. They don't want to hear other people or products criticized. They simply want to know why yours are better.

Closing Strategies for the S

The rules for closing with the steadfast are fairly simple and straightforward. Here they are:

- Let them try before they buy.
- Give them numbers of satisfied customers they can call on their own.
- Give them the opportunity to make a deposit.
- Give a money-back guarantee whenever possible.

That's basically it. Just be sincere and genuine and show steadfast customers that you are a hard worker, and that you're honest and loyal. That's all they really want to know.

PART 2
Advanced Chemistry

CHAPTER 11

Portrait of the Artist as a Young Businessperson

In the first part of the book, we discussed the basic formulas of sales success—all those complex nuances of behavior and personality that you need to master in order to develop better business relationships with your customers and colleagues.

Now, in this second part, we will discuss the advanced chemistry of sales and marketing, showing you how certain masters of the sales or marketing professions have learned to achieve success by integrating their entire life philosophy into their business strategies. In the following chapter, I will introduce you to several very influential sales and marketing professionals who have agreed to share their "secrets of success." The three relatively young adults I have chosen to interview in this chapter—Chris McCabe, Carey Earle, and Tom Livaccari —are truly accomplished in the art of networking and building business relationships.

Since I think their life stories speak for themselves, I will preface each interview by describing how I have come to know each of these individuals and how I have observed consistent patterns of professionalism in them all the time I have known them.

SUCCESS PORTRAIT

Chris McCabe
Industry Vice President
Reed Exhibition Companies
Norwalk, Connecticut

Chris McCabe, age thirty-two, recently left his post as manager of Integrated Marketing for *Money* magazine, after accepting a position as industry vice president for Reed Exhibition Companies, the largest trade show company in the world. Among his other accomplishments at *Money,* Chris helped create a series of successful strategies to integrate the marketing of the magazine with the sale of books published by its parent company, Time Warner.

At Reed Exhibition Companies, Chris is one of a handful of top executives who are orchestrating some of the world's largest trade shows. As usual, Chris rose to this challenge by studying his industry in depth, reading both academic and business books in order to become a scholar of the markets he served.

When I first met Chris, I was senior editor of *LEADERS,* and Chris was hired to sell advertising. He was only about twenty-three then, and I was in my late twenties. My first impression was that Chris was simply one of the nicest guys I had ever met—funny, enthusiastic, curious, friendly, open-minded, soft-spoken, humble, and genuinely interested in everyone and everything. He rarely talked about himself or his own interests but was continually walking around, asking five million questions of everyone he met about things that *they* were interested in. But besides being curious, he seemed to exhibit a natural and innate enthusiasm for other people, and he also seemed to be genuinely interested in everything that other people had to say about themselves or *their* interests.

If I had to pick one word to describe Chris's outlook and persona back then, it would be "delighted." He seemed to be *delighted* by every new fact or discovery he made. He also seemed to be *delighted* by learning. And because of this, he was always delightful to be around.

I will never forget when Chris made his first big sale. The computer telecommunications industry was in an accelerated wave of development, and Chris wanted to sell some advertising space to Hayes Microcomputer, one of the leading modem manufacturers. For several weeks, Chris read everything he could get his hands on about modems. He read so much that I felt he was prepared to write some scientific papers on the subject, and I asked him if he felt like he was a little *overprepared.* After all, he simply wanted to sell some ad space.

"You can never be too prepared," he said.

"Why's that?" I asked.

"Well," he said, "you never know when you might get a call from the president of the company."

"Do you really think Dennis Hayes, the president of the company, is going to call you about an advertisement?" I asked.

"Probably not," he said. "But I always want to *prepare* myself for speaking to the president, just in case it ever happens. You see, if I go through the mental exercise of preparing myself to speak to the president, even if it never happens, I'll always know I have my ducks in a row, no matter what."

Needless to say, I was very impressed, but I still didn't think that Chris, a junior account executive fresh out of college, was going to get called by the president of a major high-technology computer company about a possible magazine ad.

A few days later, I was visiting Chris in his office and the receptionist buzzed through.

"Chris, Hayes Microcomputer on line twelve."

"Great. Who is it?"

"Dennis Hayes."

Chris smiled. I was stunned. Chris picked up the phone.

I sat there dumbfounded and listened as Chris carried on a scientific discussion about modem technology for almost an hour with the president of the world's leading modem manufacturer.

He was leaning forward the entire time, his face lit with interest and excitement, and he kept saying things like, "You know, the thing that fascinates me most about your company, Mr. Hayes, is . . ." and "You know, Mr. Hayes, the thing that excites me most about the future of modem technology is . . ."

By the time Chris got off the phone, he had sold a year's worth of two-page advertising spreads to Dennis Hayes, who had decided to respond to a letter Chris had written to him simply because he was impressed with Chris's writing style and knowledge of the subject matter.

Shortly thereafter, Chris was promoted to director of advertising.

That's how Chris behaved when he was twenty-three. And he hasn't changed much at all, thank goodness. If anything, he is even more focused today.

But before we get to the meat and potatoes of Chris's "secrets of success," I want to describe his background a little bit more. As you will see, there may be a genetic component to his talent. Chris's dad, Charles McCabe, is also one of the friendliest and most unassuming people you will ever meet, despite the fact that many people in marketing describe him as one of the most brilliant marketing minds in the nation. McCabe recently retired as executive vice president of corporate marketing for the Chase Manhattan Bank.

Now, Chris's father has his own consulting company, The Hanover Group, and he is one of the most highly sought-after marketing experts in the country, in addition to being a commissioner for the city of New York. He has also raised a son who is continuing his father's legacy of social consciousness, community involvement, and marketing brilliance.

But what's the formula? How did he do it? What's the secret to this family's success?

Just listen to Chris explain it all in his own words, as he has volunteered to explain the salesmanship secrets he has learned with the readers of this book.

D.S. Chris, how does one become a master marketing and salesperson, like yourself and your dad? What's the secret?

C.M. Well, I think the first thing to remember is that the turtle never gets anywhere until he sticks his head out of the shell. You have to have confidence in your abilities, and learn not to be afraid or intimidated by new situations. Your first step is simply to go out there in the world to see what needs exist that you can address with your products and services. But you can't possibly find out what the needs are until you get out there and ask a lot of questions.

Then you have to ask yourself: If I do go out there and research a particular need, what kind of solutions might I offer if I find the need does, in fact, exist? That is to say, you can't go out exploring a potential problem or need unless you first think that you might be able to do something about this problem or need after you've analyzed it.

The other important behavior and mindset you have to cultivate is that of the student and the teacher. When you approach any customer, no matter who it is, you have to let that customer know that they are the teacher and you are the student. You listen to the customer. You take mental notes or real notes. You let the customer tell you what they need, or what's wrong, or what they need fixed. Then you come back to them with a solution.

The message you bring is always this: Dear Customer, if you will divulge enough information, then I can probably help you. And I will sit here and listen as long as it takes for you to divulge it.

So the two main starting points for success in salesmanship are these:

First, you have to overcome any sense of intimidation or fear of failure. Just force yourself, no matter how hard it might be, to simply ignore any negative thoughts that intrude on your mental space any time of the day or night. Put them completely out of your head. Because, the fact of the matter is you're not going to fail, you're going to do great, just as long as you stick to the basics.

Second, you have to constantly present yourself humbly, to everyone, like a student who has just shown up to learn his new lesson for the day. And make it clear to every person you meet, especially your customers, that you want to be their partner—that is, you want to play a humble partnership role in helping them to solve their problems and make their life better.

Those are the two basic secrets. If you just keep doing that every day, you're well on your way to success.

D.S. You and I both know that there are some people like yourself, your father, or our friend Tom Livaccari, vice president of ICon, who simply project an aura of trust. When people like you or them walk into a room, it feels like something good is about to happen. Then there are other people who walk into a room and leave you immediately suspicious. You know something's up, you don't trust them, and you would never buy anything from them in a million years. But not a word has been spoken. What's the difference between those two types of people?

C.M. What you're talking about is a complex and sophisticated question about human psychology and human relationships. Let me try to answer it this way:

Everything you do in life has to do with your history. It takes a while to build relationships, a sense of trust with people. If you want to be really successful in life, I think, you should get into the habit of presenting yourself calmly and humbly to every person you meet, all the time, whether that person is your customer, your wife, your child, or a stranger on the street.

If you do that all the time, people are going to begin to trust you. But the really complex and, I guess, neat part of it all is that this kind of behavior eventually becomes a part of your character—and then even strangers will begin to sense that you're a trustworthy person before they've even had a chance to talk with you. Because of the aura you project. And most people are highly intuitive about these kinds of things.

So your history is very important. What you do to other people, how you behave, it all comes back sooner or later. Therefore, the way you behave around other people can either come back to make you more successful, or it will come back to haunt you.

The next part of the interview reminded me of a conversation I had with Chris a long time ago, back when he was in his early twenties. We were walking through Central Park and we were talking about similar themes. I can't remember the exact words he used then, but it went something like this:

"You know those kind of people who you just seem to trust from the word go?" he asked, as we were walking through the park. "I think they're the kind of people who have been treating other people well their entire lives, while also being kind of humble about it all.

"But those other people, the ones who scare you the moment you're in their presence, even before they've said a single word—those are the people who have been running around being blowhards their entire life, or being rude and self-centered. And you can't hide who you are. You can't hide where you've been, what you've done, how you've behaved. People just know. They can sense these things.

"So I think you have to build up a reputation for being a person who is there to make everyone's life better, and not a person just focused solely on himself. That's the attitude most people respect. And when you have that history, you can get positive results every time you walk into a room, because you're carrying positive energy."

This conversation in the park was not the last time I heard Chris vocalize his "moral philosophy" on the difference between professional and unprofessional business matters. Like most truly successful and centered people, he doesn't walk around just mouthing words that sound nice.

Instead, he actually *believes* in ethical principles *and* he has practiced what he preaches *from the very beginning.*

Therefore, it is no small wonder that his advice today is almost exactly the same thing he was saying that day in Central Park when he was twenty-three. Notice the similarity of thoughts between the Central Park discussion ten years ago and the following words he spoke when interviewed recently:

C.M. So my first piece of advice to people who want to be successful is this: Make it a daily habit to present yourself to the entire world as a humble student and a person who is thinking of something more than himself. Keep doing that every day and in a couple of years, you will be successful and you'll sleep well, too.

My next piece of advice is that when you're meeting a person for the first time, just walk in, smile, look them in the eye, lay your cards on the table, and tell them the truth. Just tell them why you're there and what you want and what you can do for them. It's that simple, really.

Body language is important, too. It's a complicated science, but basically you want to demonstrate that you're confident, but that you're also *deferring* to the other person. You can't come on too strong. Never sit at the head of the table when you're with a customer. Let the customer sit at the head of the table. Because no matter how you say it, in body language, or in words, you have to tell that customer—hey, for the next half hour, or hour, you're the man, or you're the woman. You're the star. You're the hero. I'm just hear to listen.

D.S. Although your father is an extremely modest man, there's no question about the fact that he's part of the elite and chosen few in the world of marketing. He's a marketing master's master—part of the Mt. Olympus crowd. What did you learn from him? What did he teach you?

C.M. My dad is a pretty special guy, and it's easy for other people to see that, too. I think it's because he treats almost all other people the same way he treats his own family. He goes out of his way to help anybody, no matter what station of life they're in. If anyone crosses his path and he thinks he can help them, he does.

And that segues right into his whole theory of networking. He always taught me that the more people you can help, and I mean *genuinely* help, not just so you can get a favor, the more people you will have on your side as you go through life. And the more people you have on your side, the better off you'll be. And someday, somehow, somewhere down the road, all those people you have helped along the way are going to come back to you and make your own life easier.

That's my father's philosophy in a nutshell. That's essentially what he taught me. And my experience so far has proved to me that he's a very wise man.

D.S. I remember once that your father wrote a letter to the editor while we were at *LEADERS* and gave his impression about success. He said a well-balanced life is composed of three factors: God, grades, and gruel. "If you have too much of either," he said, "you become an egghead, fat, or a religious fanatic. But if you have just enough of each," he added, "you become a successful person." Are those your values, too?

C.M. Well, that's a hard quote to follow—God, grades, and gruel! But in terms of values, yes, I think you have to know where your priorities are. This is nothing new, but it's about family and health and enjoying the short time you have here on earth.

You have to look at life as this period where you're simply *here* and you have to deal with other people and make the best of it. To make the best of it, you have to remember the important things, your family, your friends, your health—and your job is just a means of getting through it all. You also have to remember to have fun while doing it as well. The same thing applies to school or anything else, any goal you want to achieve.

Religion is important to me, too. I'm pretty religious. I wouldn't say I'm a fanatic, but I definitely believe there's a higher being. And I think there are consequences attached to your actions. You create your level of positive energy and your potential influence with people over a long period of time by the way you treat each individual human being who crosses your path each and every day, even when you think no one else is looking.

But, in a nutshell, my philosophy is just to be positive and remember that what goes around comes around. That's all you need to remember, really.

D.S. Chris, you're one of the most successful people your age that I know, especially in marketing. How important is success to you?

C.M. There is nothing in the world that's so important or alluring that it would make me want to sell my soul. I'm not going to compromise myself for anybody. Besides that, I don't think wealth or success or power are the ultimate goals you should have. I mean they're nice, I suppose, if you achieve them honestly, but not if you have to earn them at the expense of having your health, your family, your integrity, or a lot of good friends.

D.S. What are the principal techniques and strategies you use to convince your potential customers to trust you more?

C.M. Homework. You have to let the customer know you've been doing your homework, while at the same time conveying the sense of that student-teacher relationship we talked about earlier. You should always seek your customer's counsel and advice on things, too. But this is where it gets tricky. You have to let the customers feel that they're educating you, but not that they're having to do your homework for you. It's a delicate balance. You have to do enough homework to make them feel like you're not wasting their time, but at the same time make them feel like you can't possibly get the big picture of the problem without their expertise.

Then, when you've done all that, you leave them with the following words: "Wow, that's great Mr. or Mrs. So-and-So. Now, with this extra valuable information that you've just given me, I feel really confident that I can come back and help you achieve some of your goals. So I really appreciate you sharing your thoughts and time with me. I couldn't have done it without you." Of course, there are many words you can use to convey that message, but that's the magic message you want to convey. That's the secret recipe everyone is looking for, in terms of salesmanship. It's a pretty simple recipe, but it works.

D.S. Do you use this student-teacher approach with everyone? Even the occasional obnoxious egomaniac we all run into from time to time?

C.M. No, I don't use it with everyone, but when I walk into a room, meeting someone for the first time, that's the approach I intend to use *first*. But if I can tell in the first ten seconds that this approach won't work, I reach into my hip pocket and pull out a few little rehearsed nuggets of the "Here's what I can do for you immediately" variety.

Ideally, you want to use the first approach, though, because it's consultative, and the more information you have up front, the better prepared you will be to help them later.

But if you can tell that the person plays it close to the vest, tell them one or two things you can do for them immediately and then see where that takes you.

If the customer is not willing to share any information with you at all, then you're probably wasting your time. Cut bait and move on to another prospect.

But if you can get them the slightest bit excited about anything, like improving their productivity, or getting their boss to like them more, then you know you're onto something.

So basically, you have your quick and easy Shake & Bake approach, which is the student-teacher approach, and your Panning for Gold approach. Those are your two basic sales approaches.

D.S. What do you do when you're not getting anywhere with a customer? Any magical sentences to use?

C.M. Yes. If I find myself being stonewalled or not making any progress with a potential customer at all, I always ask the same question. I ask, "Well Mr. or Mrs. So-and-So, how would you handle this situation if you were me? I'm feeling stumped. I don't think I'm getting anywhere and I don't think I'm telling you what you need to know." That one sentence works almost all of the time. Try it. It makes them think.

D.S. Can you tell us about the worst sales call you ever made?

C.M. I don't want to tell you where it happened, but I can say it happened early in my career and I had not done my homework before getting on the phone to call a very important potential customer. I quickly learned that when you do this, your ignorance immediately rears its ugly head. I found out what it is like to feel extremely embarrassed and stupid. I realized that I had just lost a very important chance to get something done with this person for a very long time. It was embarrassing for everyone, I think, even the other guy, the potential customer. All because I was young and green and didn't know the ropes and decided to call someone up without taking the time to study the issue first. I don't want to experience that feeling of stupidity and ignorance ever again, if I can help it. Let me just leave it at that.

D.S. What's your top-five list of ways to be successful at sales, for all young budding salespeople who want to be the best they can be?

C.M.

1. Don't just work hard; work smart. Integrate ideas and people. Build your ideas and plans carefully.

2. Know what your boss's needs are, and what makes him or her tick.

3. Really understand the role your company's products or services play with your customers and why they are valuable.

4. Monitor, as best you can, your colleagues, and try to do things just as good, if not better.

5. Just show up at work every day and try to find the silver lining. I know it sounds like a cliché, but it's really important.

D.S. What's your favorite quote?

C.M. "People who look down on other people never get looked up to." I don't know who said it, but it's the most important concept I know.

D.S. How important is it to have your Marketing Identity speech committed to memory?

C.M. It's critical. You should know what you're selling like the back of your hand.

So, those are the guiding principles of Chris McCabe, industry vice president of Reed Exhibition Companies, an outstanding example, I think, of what most truly successful young marketing people should try to be like.

SUCCESS PORTRAIT

Carey Earle
CEO
Harvest Consulting Group
New York, New York

In terms of being a marketing whiz, an earth-shaker, a shaker-upper, a trendsetter, a future maker, and an unstoppable competitor in the world of marketing, Carey Earle has earned her reputation primarily by being a good listener and a hard, responsive worker who gives her customers what they need. Soft-spoken and straightforward, Carey has developed a style of relating to her customers that is best described in her own words: "I try to let my customers know right from the start that I am a hands-on person in a hands-off world." That simple strategy has helped Carey quickly establish herself as a rising young star in the world of electronic marketing and strategic consulting.

As CEO of Harvest Consulting Group in New York City, Carey's got real chemistry—and an impressive list of Fortune 500 clients are asking her to help them refine and then distill the magic chemistry of their own marketing efforts. If I can make you understand how Carey's mind works, then I think you will understand why some of the nation's largest companies have chosen to work with her instead of the larger, big-name advertising agencies.

The first person who mentioned Carey's name to me said, "Man, I have got to put you in touch with this woman named Carey Earle. You'll just love her. She's awesome." We met at a coffee shop for breakfast on the Upper East Side of New York, decided to become partners, and then developed the rough sketch of a training program for increasing creativity in the work-place before we finished our oatmeal—a mere forty-five minutes into our first meeting. Carey is a superb strategist and has masterminded market-ing initiatives for many companies. I have become increasingly fascinated by the way she works, the way her mind operates, and the way people are so drawn to her.

When I first met Carey in front of that coffee shop, I was bowled over by her aura of simplicity and modesty. Carey, who grew up on a Vermont dairy farm, is the picture of health. A fresh-faced, energetic, humble, cheerful, exuberant, and powerfully levelheaded woman, she has no discernible level of pretension or arrogance—which, as I have mentioned before, seems to be one of the hallmark traits of some of the most successful people I have had the chance to meet. As with many successful people, she has not let her numerous achievements cloud her personality. A mas-ter salesperson and competitor in the new frontier of electronic marketing, Carey is clearly aggressive, but you hardly notice because of her calm, soft-spoken, easygoing manner. She's very down-to-earth. She laughs a lot. But you must watch out for her if you're in the same business, because she literally obliterates her competition—softly, but surely.

"Softly" is the operative word because, as Carey explains, most compa-nies are becoming increasingly disenchanted with loudmouthed, pushy salespeople. "Times are changing in the corporate world," Carey says. "Being credentialed isn't good enough anymore. You have to be smart *and* easy to work with. One of the comments I hear from many people I've worked with, in fact, is 'You're so easy to work with, Carey! That's why we want you around.'

"The era of the out-of-control ego is coming to a close," Carey adds. No-body wants it anymore. Attitude means nothing to the real leaders of today. People are sick of the whole attitude thing. It's intelligence and talent and connectivity that win you customers, the ability to listen and connect with people on an honest level.

"Corporate culture used to be all about power suits and nice little leather portfolios," Carey continues. "The entire era represented a triumph of form over substance—people were more concerned with how a presentation looked than what it said. But now the deck has been reshuffled. American Express is a great example. They now have a casual dress-down five-days-a-week policy in the American Express tower.

"What this means is significant. . . . It means that your suit no longer means anything and you will be judged by your brain, your talent, and your ability to work with other people. And also by your sense of self and your willingness to make the customer look good. I cannot overemphasize the importance of that concept. . . . If anybody were to ask me what my secret of success was, I would say this: I bend over backwards and work myself to the bone trying to make my clients look good.

"But making the customer look good involves a lot of things—especially to people inside the same organization, if you're serving business units. Doing one clever marketing campaign or ad spot isn't enough to make your customer look good. You have to use the rest of your brain, too. So many times an ad agency will think it has done its job because it came up with one compelling campaign. But the real issue is how do we pull an entire marketing strategy through an organization. Anyone can sit around and think big thoughts, but who's going to take the big thought to the mat and make it real?

"Oftentimes I am stunned when I start talking to some middle management executives about their need for a new marketing campaign. I ask them to tell me what the four primary marketing messages of the company are and they say they don't know, because it isn't part of their job. When I ask them, modestly, what their job might happen to be, they invariably report that their job is to 'look at the big picture.' I don't know what to say to such people. What kind of big picture can you possibly be working on if you don't even know your company's four primary marketing messages?"

According to Carey, people who don't understand, or don't care to even take the time to understand, their company's primary marketing messages—no matter what their executive title is—are beginning to annoy everyone and shouldn't count on holding their jobs very much longer. Most companies, she says, are increasingly coming to realize that important members of the corporate team must begin to show some concern over the issue of integration—how all marketing messages are connected, even internal marketing messages, and how the organization functions as a living marketing organism. "You see, if you want to really be successful, remember this one thing—people need you to help them integrate. Fulfill that need and you'll have all the customers you can handle."

But how do you go about filling those needs? Carey advises, "In order to accurately fill your customers' needs you have to constantly ask yourself, 'How can I help my business customers explain how each element of the marketing initiative is related to all others—existing or planned? How can I help my customers show the world that they are on the ball and thinking of the long-term strategy?' This means building a seamless stream of effective communication."

When I asked Carey to describe her first "big sale" she leapt at the subject with relish, enthusing that she could remember it "as if it were yesterday."

"I was working with Grey Advertising and I had the chance to make a pitch for a large consulting firm. This would have been a prestigious account for Grey because at that time they didn't have any accounts in the professional services area. And they wanted more business-to-business work and more technology work. So, because of my background, they asked me to spearhead the team.

"A couple of weeks before the meeting, I found out that a woman I used to work with at Burson-Marsteller knew someone there, and so I called her and asked her if there was anything I should know before going in about their corporate culture and the success or lack of success they had had with people in the past. And I also asked her how she would like to be presented to.

"When I asked her what had gone wrong with their last agency, if anything, she came right out and told me that their problems with people in the past boiled down to two things: First, they gave really poor service. The client didn't feel valued and responded to. Second, they didn't seem to know their business. Immediately, I knew what to do and I got very energized and wrote most of the presentation in one night. But I knew that what was going to sell them was not the proposal, but the message behind the proposal. And I knew the decision to buy the proposal was going to be a democratic vote among a wide range of marketing professionals, the senior management, and junior and senior executives, people responsible for helping to get publicity, and other people responsible for market development. Therefore, I knew that they wanted to know how our proposal and our team would help them all work together in an integrated fashion.

"I also realized that the key to the sale was the fact that they all felt betrayed by their last agency, which came in giving a song and dance about being global and wonderful, but didn't deliver, didn't stand by their product, didn't get down into the trenches and get dirty. They didn't help them understand their positioning or their key marketing messages. I knew this was going to be a personal sell. So when we sat down around the boardroom table, I gave them personal references to call from people I had worked with who would testify to my follow-through, and testify to the fact that I got down in the trenches and did whatever needed to be done until the goal was accomplished and the client was completely satisfied.

"Then I ended my presentation by giving the following speech. I said: 'Folks, this is all about chemistry. And I don't want you to choose us as an agency if you don't feel comfortable that you can work with me, that we can be sitting together on a desk at midnight, crunching through documents. That's what this is about. And that's why some relationships with agencies fail, when the chemistry and the trust and the belief are not there.

"'Because this isn't about business; this is about trust,' I said. 'We've all got the same level of intelligence, we've all got the same computers, but some of us actually care about giving it everything we've got. Because we care about making you look as good as you can possibly look to the people that count, inside this company and out on the street. And I'm someone who knows enough about you to know where you're trying to go, and who will do anything to help you prioritize jobs in order to get there. And that's what makes us different from the other agencies. I am that person. The person who cares about your business and will get inside it.'

"And when I said that, every head in the room was nodding and nodding and nodding, just a roomful of deep slow nods, and everyone was making eye contact with me, and I knew in that moment that we had the account. I had won. Hands down. The other guys were finished.

"When we got the account, they sent a case of French champagne. Inside the case was a note that said: 'This was one of the best presentations that we've seen in our marketing careers.'"

In a nutshell, that's Carey Earle. That's how she operates, and that's how she keeps steadily increasing her level of success with customers.

One final note of encouragement to all creative types out there—Carey reports that at American Express and other corporations she is working closely with, creativity and individuality are becoming increasingly attractive. Companies are looking less for people with "assembly-line" Ivy League backgrounds and more for people with a wide variety of experiences.

So, if you ever wondered when your day would come as a creative, individualistic, slightly iconoclastic type, you might rest more comfortably knowing that some very successful firebrands like Carey Earle honestly believe your day is now.

SUCCESS PORTRAIT

Tom Livaccari
Director of Sales and Marketing
Dennis Interactive
New York, New York

In 1964, David Mayer and Herbert M. Greenberg published a now-classic article in the *Harvard Business Review* titled "What Makes a Great Salesman." Ironically, this was the same year that Thomas J. Livaccari was conceived. In retrospect, some marketing experts familiar with Tom's behavior consistently agree that there must have been some kind of planetary alignment at the moment Greenberg and Mayer conceived their article and the Livaccaris conceived their son. Because what Alfia and Dominick produced, in the opinion of many experts, is something akin to a Robo-salesman, a kind of human selling machine that cannot be stopped by ordinary weapons.

At the time of this writing, Tom was director of sales and marketing for Dennis Interactive, one of the nation's leading interactive software development companies and a subsidiary of Dennis Publishing, the largest independently owned publishing company in the United Kingdom. Previously, Tom was a sales executive for CompuServ before he quit his job to help create and take public ICon New Media and create (with Earle and others) the pioneering online magazine *Word,* which was the Internet's first independent, non-print-based publication supported by advertising. As fate would have it, Tom was working for CompuServe when the World Wide Web was still an idea—before he left this position to help create ICon.

"There were a few of us back then who saw it coming, this idea of the World Wide Web," Tom says. "The Web wasn't even in existence at that point, but we glimpsed the possibilities, and so we all quit our safe jobs and went out on a limb. I guess the rest is history now."

To say the least. Tom and his peers, such as Carey Earle, might have something in common, I think, with Christopher Columbus, Amelia Earhart, Charles Lindbergh, Thomas Edison, and other bold pioneers. While naysayers may have originally scoffed at them for taking "flights of fancy" about the possibilities of the computer, they actually ended up discovering and building new worlds in the universe of electronic marketing. Because of these young pioneers (most of them were in their twenties at the time), the world has been radically changed. Virtual communities, virtual businesses, and even a kind of virtual consciousness was created.

Who can imagine life now without the Internet?

Now ponder this: In the beginning, Tom and his peers were out there on the streets of New York selling advertising space for electronic media products that didn't even exist yet. That's right. Think about that from a sales standpoint: Tom sold advertising for *Word* magazine before the magazine even existed—when it was still just an idea. On a chutzpah scale of one to ten, that's got to be a ten. How did he do it? He had four things:

1. A great idea

2. Nuclear-powered enthusiasm for that idea

3. A desire to conquer

4. Empathy, or a greater-than-average ability to identify with his customers

Mayer and Greenberg cite the last two items in my list as the two most important things a great salesperson can have, and I, too, certainly believe these qualities are paramount for all businesspeople. I also think that the first two points are equally important.

When I met Tom, he had just been hired as an advertising executive at *LEADERS* magazine, brought in at about the same time as my good friend Chris McCabe. The first day Tom came into my office to introduce himself, he was talking about the future of the human race. He couldn't sit still. His smile seemed to be bigger than his whole head. Although it seemed like he had drunk about twenty cups of coffee, he swore he hadn't touched a drop of caffeine, because it was too early and he didn't want to get wound up too soon. Every time I found a space to open my mouth and interject a comment, he started waving his hands and moving around, saying things like: "Yeah, yeah, that's what I'm saying. I'm talking about the future of the human race, here. I'm talking about money, I'm talking about music, I'm talking about computers, I'm talking about working smart and acting smart. I'm talking about women, man. Because women are beautiful. I love 'em. I love all of 'em. I like the way they look, I like the way they think, I like the way they smell. I love women. I got to have 'em. They're incredible. Don't you think women are incredible? I gotta hug every single woman on the planet. Women are the future of the human race. Women and computers. An international network. Mind to mind. Body to body. You hear what I'm saying? That's it. That's the thing. That's what I'm saying. You're absolutely right."

I somehow felt that I was in the presence of a nuclear-powered marketing cyborg, some kind of plutonium-fueled alien from Planet Sales. In the years since, I have seen Tom cool down a little bit—from 1166 degrees Kelvin to 1165 degrees, which is at least a start. Along the way, Tom built a resumé that seemed to fit together like a puzzle as his career in sales and marketing progressed.

Tom climbed the sales and marketing ladder pretty quickly. But how did he do it? In his evolution from salesperson to marketing executive, how did he cultivate those four essential qualities we talked about earlier?

Let's take a brief look.

A Great Idea

In business, you generally know you have a great idea if you have been able to successfully fill out your Marketing Identity Worksheet and it all sounds good. If you would buy your products or services yourself, then chances are you have a great idea. If you wouldn't spend your own money on your own products or services, chances are you don't.

Enthusiasm

Maybe Tom Livaccari and others like him were just born with an inordinate amount of enthusiasm—that fiery energy of spirit that is part of the life energy Eastern philosophers and doctors call *chi*—but I actually think that such a high-energy level of enthusiasm can be cultivated.

The secret recipe to creating and maintaining enthusiasm is not at all difficult, according to most of the enthusiastic, energetic people I know. First, you must always force yourself to stay positive, no matter what. Positive thinking, which requires effort, creates positive energy. Negative thinking, which requires no effort (just like staying in bed requires no effort), creates negative energy and gloominess. Second, you must stay focused on your Marketing Identity Worksheet and refuse to let negative, weak, and annoying people drag you off the board.

Then, make an effort to rise early. Be nice to yourself. Also be nice to other people. Help people as often as you can. Try to make at least one positive contribution to the life of another human being each day. Also, eat healthy. Don't drink or smoke too much, if you drink or smoke at all. Tell the truth. Enjoy your sexuality. Don't be puritanical. Live life to the fullest. Have adventures. Drink from the cup of life abundantly.

If you do these things, you will maintain a high level of enthusiasm—that sparkling quality of life energy that magnetizes others and makes them want to gather around you.

Desire to Conquer/Competitive Spirit

Timothy O'Connor, division sales manager for EBI Medical Systems, a major manufacturer and distributor of medical supplies, told me a funny story about his team of salespeople when we met for dinner one night in Charlotte, North Carolina, during a podiatric medical conference.

"I love my salespeople," O'Connor said. "These people are so competitive, it's unbelievable.

"Even though some of these people are making over $100,000 a year, all you have to do is throw them the littlest bone and they pump up the volume even more.

"For example, not too long ago, I offered a batch of Blockbuster gift certificates to the salespeople who could increase sales by a certain amount in a small period of time. For people who are making over $100,000 a year, a $5 gift certificate isn't much, but it was like throwing out a football into the middle of the Super Bowl. You have never seen people scramble so fast. Everybody wanted those gift certificates. . . . The point is it was a chance to win—to prove they were better—so they fought tooth and nail, in a friendly competitive way, to get them.

"That's the kind of 'desire to conquer' people are talking about when they talk about what makes great salespeople. Good salespeople just want to win all the time—they don't care how big or small the prize might be. They just always want to prove that they're better than anyone else at what they do."

I happen to know one of those fiercely competitive salespeople on the EBI sales force that Tim is talking about. His name is Wayne Rouse. Wayne is a poster hero for the whole humble sales philosophy I have been talking about in this book. For while Wayne's sales manager, Tim O'Connor, describes him as fiercely competitive, highly driven, and a dynamite salesperson, that's not how he comes across. In fact, what you see from the customer's standpoint is exactly the opposite. Just like Tom Livaccari, Wayne Rouse, on a sales call, comes across as the most soft-spoken, calm, unpretentious, and humble person you have ever met.

So, the desire to conquer may be very important—but master salespeople keep that desire carefully concealed, from a behavioral point of view, as soon as they enter a client's office. People like Wayne and Tom might be highly competitive, but the important thing is you'd never know it.

Empathy

By definition, empathy is the ability to understand why another person is feeling the way he or she is feeling. Empathy is a higher-quality emotion than sympathy. If you are sympathetic, you feel sorry for someone's troubles. If you are empathetic, you genuinely understand what another human being's troubles are all about, and why he or she might feel sad or confused, because you feel that person's troubles yourself.

Empathy is also less injurious than sympathy. Sympathy has an unhealthy component to it sometimes—because if often means that you have allowed yourself to become entangled in another person's emotions, usually without even understanding the other's emotions to begin with. You may begin to feel the other person's emotions—anger, sadness, distress—and even resent the other person for dragging you into the morass of his or her negative feelings. So feeling sympathetic isn't always a good thing.

When you are empathetic, on the other hand, it means that you have entered a state of understanding and compassion for another person, but you are not allowing your emotions to become entangled with theirs. You remain concerned and compassionate and helpful, but emotionally separate. It is usually a more healthy place to be.

As a salesperson, empathy might just be one of your biggest assets—if not the biggest—as Mayer and Greenberg suggest in their 1966 article. Empathy is what makes most people like you, because the single most driving need of most human beings, regardless of their personality or behavioral style, is the need or desire to be understood. So if people think you understand them, they *like* you. That on its own is a great benefit for salespeople—and remember, all businesspeople are salespeople first and foremost. And empathy has an added benefit for salespeople: If you are good at figuring out what is bothering a person—that is, what their problems are—you can usually be just as good at helping them solve those problems.

Now this is where the rubber meets the road, so pay attention: Most highly empathetic people are described by their friends as people who listen more than they talk.

Got it? See the connection between empathy and sales success?

Take Tom Livaccari, for example. I know very few businesspeople Tom's age in New York who have as many friends as he does. He has thousands of friends all over the place in top positions at some of the world's leading companies. Now that Tom has matured and has learned to keep a lid on his boiling pot of energy, almost everyone I have ever met who is a friend of Tom's says exactly the same things:

> "I have never heard him say a negative word about anybody! He always finds something good to say about everyone!"

"He's always so positive!"

"He's so full of life!"

"He's such a good listener!"

"He's interested in everything!"

"He doesn't seem to have a judgmental bone in his body!"

I wonder if there is also a connection between those observations, which one hears over and over again, and the fact that Tom might have more friends than anybody his age in New York.

Now, salespeople, pay attention: Imagine that you are on the telephone trying to sell something to Tom. You would think that with all of this non-judgmental empathy on his side that you would be able to sell him any-thing. Wrong.

We must never forget that businesspeople (who are all salespeople at heart), put much tougher expectations on other salespeople than they do on the rest of humanity, because it's their profession you're talking about—the same way doctors seem to put higher expectations for professionalism on other doctors. As a matter of fact, Tom says that many other salespeo-ple drive him nuts, just from their sheer incompetence.

So, without further delay, let's give Tom the floor.

How to Be a Winner—Not a Loser

"I believe very strongly in the quality of empathy you have been talking about in this book," Tom says, "but there's a quality of empathy that goes beyond the professional description of salesperson.

"Every person in sales and marketing has to be a consultant, that's the image you have to have of yourself—a professional consultant. You must carry that image with you no matter what business you are in, or what you are selling. You almost have to think of yourself as a doctor. You walk into every customer's office the way a doctor would walk into a patient's room. You are there to diagnose the problem. You are an expert and you know what you're doing. You are there to recommend the 'treatment' or product or service that your customer needs. Just like a real physician, you would never in your wildest dreams try to push something on the patient or client that they didn't actually need.

"It is this new approach to professionalism in sales that is truly changing all of the rules. If you want to be a professional, you have to act and behave like one. Your reputation will be obvious as soon as you walk in the door. You are there to provide. And to provide the kind of guidance that is truly professional, you have to study. Just as a doctor sits at home at the end of the day reading the *New England Journal of Medicine,* you have to sit under your own reading light learning more about your customers' businesses. That's what professionalism in sales and marketing is all about.

"When I think of great salespeople, I think of giants like Richard Branson, whom all of us admire, and . . . of people like Carey Earle.

"What makes Carey great is that she really genuinely does care about her clients. That's what she projects to anyone who does business with her— that she really does care about them and their businesses. You would not believe the amount of work the woman does, as well, in learning and researching her customer's needs. She's a scholar. And those traits that Carey possesses are key traits to have if you are going to be a successful salesperson in the future.

"Because of my position, people are trying to sell me things all the time. But it's funny, you can pick out a good salesperson and a bad salesperson in the first ten seconds. The bad ones really turn you off. You never want to talk to them again.

"The bad ones give you the impression that they're reading from a script, or giving you the same old song and dance they give everyone else. Bad salespeople always give you the impression that they know nothing about your business beyond the superficial.

"Another turnoff is when people are aloof, and don't seem to have a genuine interest in what you are talking about. That usually ties into the next point. They don't listen. They do all the talking and they just don't listen. That's an age-old issue with salespeople. It seems like people would have learned by now, with all of the salesmanship training seminars out there. But still, so many salespeople just don't get it. They won't shut up. They still insist on doing all of the talking.

"Another big turnoff is they don't do what they say they're going to do. If they say they're going to follow up with more information, or a report, or something like that, they don't. You expect things on a certain day, and then that day comes and goes and they don't get back to you. That's bad.

"It's all about impressions. If they make a bad first impression, that's an issue. And those are the three biggest ways I know to create a bad first impression."

So, that being said, how do you go about cultivating credentials as a sales professional and consultant? And what is the real future of marketing and salesmanship? What kinds of skills and talents will matter most as we move into the new millennium?

Tom Livaccari's Top Seven Rules for Sales Success in the New Millennium

1. Sell something you believe in.
"I guess my best sales calls, or the ones I remember with the greatest sense of accomplishment," Tom says, "were when I sold my first ads for *Word,* our online magazine, the first online magazine in the world, as a matter of fact, that didn't have a print counterpart.

"What we were doing had never been done before. We were out there pitching a brand-new concept to advertising agencies.

"I guess I felt pretty successful when I was able to sell MasterCard and Zima into something that didn't even exist, when the customer couldn't even get a feel for what the product was going to be like.

"It was a long process. It started with education. We had to teach people what the Internet was. We are talking about people who didn't even have a grasp of what the Internet was about. So first, we had to walk in and tell them what it was.

"At this point we had no prototype, no way of showing the customer what our product was going to look like. All that we had at this point was words on paper. There wasn't anything to show.

"The way that we made them feel confident in our abilities was to teach them, to show them what the future had in store. And by teaching them the subject thoroughly and carefully, we were able to build a sense of trust.

"So, at that point, when we sold $100,000 worth of ads for this yet-to-be-launched product in a new industry, that was fulfilling. It was like breaking new ground. The feeling of conquest? Yeah, it was sweet."

2. Develop an enthusiastic but elite sales style.
"With me the secret of sales is pretty basic. You come in with a big smile on your face and you show a lot of energy—but controlled energy. Not wild energy. Not manic energy. But energy under control. Controlled energy is not something that came naturally for me. It doesn't come naturally for most enthusiastic young people. But it's something you have to learn. It's something you have to practice.

"Also, you must exhibit genuineness—smiles, controlled energy, and genuineness. These are things that let people know you are not going to try and take advantage of them, take them for a ride.

"Superb salesmanship is also about being confident without being cocky. That's very important. That's what helped me when I started to sell the idea of the Internet. I was always conscious of needing to appear confident, but also very careful not to appear cocky. The first trait is winsome; the second is like the kiss of death.

"Another thing . . . is the importance of *believing* in your product. I cannot stress the importance of that. . . .

"When I went out on the street trying to sell people on this whole idea of the Internet, I walked in the door telling them that this medium was going to change the entire face of publishing. And I honestly believed it. I still do. Because it has, you see. We weren't kidding.

"And the fact that I projected such a strong belief, and coupled my belief with facts and an educational approach, led people to accept the Internet as imminent. And so they opened up their checkbooks—and started spending hundreds of thousands of dollars. On a vision eloquently described."

3. Figure out what your product or service really has to offer—not what you think it has to offer.   "In the last two years, we have learned what the Internet is best at. What we first thought it was best at and what it has actually proved itself to be best at are not the same thing.

"At first we thought the Internet would primarily be about entertainment, that we would be entertaining people on-line. But we have found that that is not the Internet's forte. Because of bandwidth issues to the home, or the lack thereof, we are finding that the Internet is not the entertainment vehicle that we thought it was.

"It's too early in the game to say we are going to compete with television . . . or the electronic game market.

"Now I look at the Internet for three main uses, personally, and I can look around me and see that this applies to other consumers as well.

"First, the Internet is best at providing information. This is most important, it seems, in the business setting. Everything I do now, personally, that requires information is done online. If I am buying a camera, if I am going on vacation, or if I am researching a company that I am going to make a sales call to, I can do it online, and I can find out information in a matter of minutes that beforehand would have taken several days.

"The Internet is all about commerce. You can buy things. It's about cutting costs. You can cut out all the unnecessary travel and entertainment expenses that go along with buying or building business-to-business relationships. It's about getting rid of the middleman.

"So I see the Internet being able to do two main things for a company: (1) cutting existing costs and (2) helping them gain market share.

"The third part of the Internet that I think is important is building communities out there based around business to business, or commerce.

"On any given day you can talk to people all over the world about your problems, your issues, your new products.

"For example, say you have a new child, and you want some information about a health-related issue pertaining to your infant. Instead of having to go to a doctor, or call your parents, or even leave your home and spend all day searching for a specialist to answer your question, you can put out your question about your baby's health on the Internet. Within minutes you will be flooded with responses from people all over the world who have been through the same thing.

"That is pretty amazing. It's a phenomenal change in reality.

"One big money-making opportunity that's coming for the Internet is the gaming industry. This might mean online gambling in some camps, but it doesn't have to. I think you will see a great emergence of multileveled, multiplayer games as the industry progresses.

"For example, you might be playing against ten or more people around the world, and each one of you will have an icon on the screen that represents you. And you will be able to converse with each other individually during the game through pop-up chat windows. That's pretty exciting. That's cool."

4. Concentrate on long-term sales success vs. short-term success.   "Basically, if you want to achieve short-term success the formula is easy. You just go out there foaming at the mouth and try to force your products on anyone you can overpower. You may do okay for a while, using that technique, but then your reputation will be ruined forever.

"It is much more advisable to focus on long-term success, which demands a more relaxed style of selling and more patience. It would behoove more sales managers and more companies to remember this, too, so that they don't put unreasonable quotas on their salespeople and force them into a state of jeopardy. You see, using the arrogant, blowhard approach to muscle your way into an account simply doesn't work in today's cautious marketplace. There might still be some arrogant, blowhard types out there, but you're seeing them less and less, because that style has become anathema to most buyers.

"Because people are jumping around from job to job so often, changing careers and that sort of thing, your success as a salesperson has to be based on long-term relationships.

"Oftentimes, because it will be so much more common to find yourself popping up in different companies every couple of years, your reputation will spread like a bad seed if you haven't been careful.

"Also, your clients will be moving around more, too, from company to company. So if you burn one bridge at company X, chances are the same buyer is going to pop up at company Y two years from now. So you have to be very careful these days.

"And because of technology, you have to be smarter and quicker as a salesperson. . . .

"Technology is making it much more difficult and much more competitive to do business, because you have to know your stuff. That's a basic tenet. Ten years ago, you knew a guy, you took him to a baseball game, you smoked some cigars, you went to a couple of bars, and then you made the sale.

"Those days are almost over. These days you have to know that guy's business inside and out. And that means you have to be as computer literate as every other young Turk out there.

"Still, you can learn from some of the old sales masters out there who still have things to teach us young guys about building relationships.

"For example, there's one old guy that comes to mind, a master salesman from the old school whom I have met. He deals mostly at the executive level and he has kept careful notes on index cards over the past twenty years about everyone he has ever talked to. So when he gets one of these guys on the phone, he knows the kids' names, he knows the guy's wife's name, he knows the wife's birthday, he knows whether the guy likes to fish or go to exotic clubs in Hong Kong. And he sells like crazy. Just because he's the master of relationships. Those are some of the techniques left over from the old school that young people today still have to master.

"So in order to be as successful as possible in sales these days, you have to integrate sophisticated knowledge in at least three distinct areas—technology, human relationships, and behavioral psychology. Your best salespeople will be conquest-minded and emphatic, yes; they will also be very skilled at building a network of relationships and keeping their own little notes on their customers, so that every client gets the personal touch. But they will also be completely up to speed with technology as a tool for client research and market research, and they will stay with the pack. They won't fall behind. That's what characterizes sales success on the street, which is the most important place for sales success to happen, anyway.

"The street-level sales strategy of any company, and the up-to-date leadership and wisdom that guides street-level sales training, taking it for granted that you have a superior product to sell, is what truly determines whether a company rises or crumbles in the face of competition and the ever-shifting perceptions of a fickle buying public. Almost everything else you hear about the nature of competitiveness is a lot of esoteric mumbo jumbo."

5. Help people for no reason. "I am also a firm believer in helping people for no reason. . . . I also try to help people on a daily basis, without a reason. I'm always putting people together, trying to help my friends make more money.

"A lot of my friends have made a lot of money as a result of me setting them up with one another. I don't expect anything in return. It's just a good thing to do. People remember you, and what goes around comes around.

"That is such a key factor of success in life that it just can't be underestimated. People remember what you do. And sooner or later it all pays off."

6. Make tons of personal phone calls. "When I worked in one of my last jobs, I got in trouble because I made a lot of personal phone calls. My sales manager, at that time, was unenlightened about reality, and so he raked me over the coals, just because I spent so much time networking on the phone. He told me it was forbidden to make personal phone calls.

"When I tried to interrupt, saying, 'But there's a reason, boss . . .' he said, 'No ifs, ands, or buts, Tom. Stop making personal calls.' And so he wrote me up in the performance evaluation.

"After that sales manager was gone, I got a new one. A real smart guy. First day on the job he comes in and says to me, 'Tom, I see you got reprimanded for making a ton of personal phone calls.' I said, 'Yes sir, I sure did.' And he said, 'Well, you'll never get reprimanded for that from me, Tom. That's the quickest way to make money. Now get back on the phone and keep up the good work.'

"Now there was an enlightened sales manager. Thank goodness he came along. Because my sales skyrocketed. In sales, you see, your network is your most powerful tool. You should make tons of personal phone calls every day. Stay plugged in. Any good sales manager knows you're supposed to, and they should encourage it. If they don't, they don't know the first thing about sales and you should start looking for a new job if money making is your goal."

7. Make every client feel you've been following his or her company for years.

"When you walk into a sales meeting and begin to talk about your knowledge of a company, it is extremely important *how* you talk about that company. You must never sound like you read about them for the first time three days ago. That's deadly.

"You must know exactly how to reference your knowledge of the company. It is imperative that you show the person you know all the news that is impacting his company and how it affects the big picture of his competitiveness and his growth.

"But it has to sound like organic knowledge, like you have been following his company for a long time.

"If you are going into a sales meeting with someone from AT&T, for example, you better have gone online and read everything about AT&T from Dow Jones news retrieval over the last year. But you never reference that stuff directly. You never say, 'Hey I was reading *The Wall Street Journal* last week and I saw that your stock price is going up.' Never. You let them know that you know what's going on, but you never reference it like that. You make your knowledge known in a subtle, low-key, professional way. If you start quoting yesterday's *Journal,* it sounds like you just went to the library five minutes ago on your way to the meeting. You want to give them the impression you've been following this stuff for years.

"So these are the major rules for successful salesmanship I know: Show enthusiasm, show empathy, show knowledge, and offer a superior product. If you just do these things, there is absolutely nothing that can stand between you and success."

CHAPTER 12

How to Integrate Sales, Marketing, and Customer Service

Billion-Dollar Tips from a Guy Who's Been There

Peace of mind is worth a lot of money.
—David A. Donatelli, vice president, Enterprise Alliances,
    EMC Corporation, Hopkington, Massachusetts

B efore we talk about what it takes to make billions of dollars and to take on giants like IBM, which is what EMC's David Donatelli and his colleagues have accomplished, I want to offer a few friendly reminders about the kind of guts and endurance required to take on the world and win.

One of the themes that I wanted to get across in this book is that most supersuccessful people whom I have met or interviewed are people just like you and me—normal and human, with strengths and weaknesses like anyone else. It is both comforting and inspirational to realize that people who have made it to some high ledge along the mountain of struggle have usually had to endure the same things the rest of us have endured from time to time—frustration, failure, short-term success that suddenly turned sour, catastrophic calamities that came out of the blue, and oftentimes unbearable pressure from without and within.

The only difference between these folks and less successful people is that they somehow found the little extra courage that is sometimes necessary to pick yourself up when you almost feel just too exhausted to keep going.

The road to success is never easy, and the journey of the successful soul—especially in business—is frequently a painful one that must be endured and experienced for what it is: an undiluted, experiential, and courageous embracing of pain and growth without anesthetic. That old adage "no pain, no gain" applies not only to weight lifting, but also to the achievement of any level of growth along the journey to success. You must be willing to endure discomfort and the sometimes agonizing process of self-examination in the clear, broad light of your own God-given mind. You must confront your fears, and your weaknesses, and your confusion. You cannot run away seeking pleasure and comfort if you want to be successful. From most of the successful people I have had the opportunity to meet and interview so far, I have learned a very valuable lesson: Almost all incredibly successful people have learned to process, deal with, and learn from the painful lessons that inevitably occur in the life of a risk-taker. And as you know, no one ever accomplished anything without taking risks.

All successful people I know are courageous people. They have not tried to hide from intense self-examination, and they have not tried to habitually anesthetize themselves, as less successful people do, as a way of escaping the growing pains of the soul that naturally occur in a goal-directed life. In other words, they have stayed strong and courageous and have faced themselves and their destinies head on. Nonsuccessful people, who obsessively prefer the world of pleasure and comfort, most often wake up and discover that they have become completely destroyed by their addiction to comfort or escapism, in whatever form their addictions take.

The young corporate leader I will profile in this chapter (age thirty-two at the time of this writing) is David Donatelli, vice president of EMC Corporation, which the *Boston Globe* named the Massachusetts Company of the Decade in 1998.

David has reached phenomenal success in the corporate world and lives the life of the successful young person usually only portrayed in movies—he sits on a corporate board with leaders who are almost twice his age. Owing to his participation in EMC's corporate leadership, David helped bring his company from $66 million in revenues in 1987 to $4 billion in 1998, partially as a result of being knighted to lead a customer service overhaul strategy when he was only twenty-five years old.

In speaking of his success, David reinforces many of the simple values that other very successful businesspeople have mentioned, namely the need to get focused, the need to get on the page and stay on the page.

David's climb up the corporate ladder has not been without personal difficulties. Several years before this book was written, when David was getting his MBA from the Kellogg School of Business while working full-time, he became very sick because he overloaded himself. Some of David's friends actually thought that he was dying of a mysterious illness. Thankfully, David's doctors finally ascertained that exhaustion and stress caused his illnesses, and so with proper rest and treatment, David was able to make a full recovery.

So, as you listen to the secrets from one of the nation's most successful and influential young executives, keep this in mind: These words of wisdom are not coming from a man who was born with a silver corporate spoon in his mouth. They come from a man who, at one point, almost worked himself to death as he struggled to meet his own personal goals and ambitions.

SUCCESS PORTRAIT

David A. Donatelli
Vice President
Enterprise Alliances, EMC Corporation
Hopkington, Massachusetts

David Donatelli joined EMC in 1987. Previous to his current position, which he has held since 1996, he was vice president of marketing for EMC's open storage group. He is currently responsible for developing partnership and alliance strategy and fostering the company's relationship with some of the world's leading technology companies, including database leaders Oracle Corp., Sybase Inc., and Informix Software. Donatelli completed his undergraduate education at Boston College and holds an MBA from the Kellogg School of Business at Northwestern University.

D.S. David, I have heard that because of your incredible people skills, your CEO has often sent you in to fix divisions of your company—even in instances in which you professed little or no knowledge of the products they were producing. That seems like an incredible testament of faith on the part of your CEO. Can you tell us a little bit about that?

D.D. I started at EMC right out of college in 1987. At the time I started, EMC was about a $66 million company. Now we're about a $4 billion company. During this time, I have done everything from running a division of customer service, to running a division of manufacturing, to running a division of engineering, to running a division of marketing. And in all those jobs, what was interesting about them is that I typically was sent in to turn around something that I knew absolutely nothing about.

D.S. How did that work?

D.D. Let me give you an example. I was hired here as a product manager, but my first large turnaround assignment was in the area of customer serivce. What happened was my CEO called me one day—he happened to be traveling in Europe—and he told me he wanted me to go look at this position in customer service, to see if I was interested in taking it. My first impression was "what did I do wrong?" But when I went over there, what I found was that there was a whole lot of employee dissatisfaction. They were very upset with the way they were being managed—the way they were being treated. At the same time, in this period in our company's history, we were about to undergo a very large product recall. And because of the fact that we were going to have to ask them to put in even more hours and do more work, tensions were beginning to skyrocket. The employees were about to go through the roof.

D.S. What specifically was it that irked the employees the most in terms of the way they were being treated?

D.D. They felt that their managers weren't representing their needs to the rest of the company. In their case, they had a need to have some new computers installed to help them do their job. They had a need to make sure that there was a structure in place to provide good customer service. These people were in charge with providing what we call Level 3 support— which means that if no one else could fix a problem it fell into these guys' laps. In order to do that well, you really need a good, organized approach through the other levels of service—but that wasn't happening. None of that was in place. So in essence, they really had no one who understood what their requirements were in order to get the job done. And they had no one who was capable of instituting the changes that needed to be made. So the CEO asked me if I would try to fix things.

D.S. How old were you at the time?

D.D. Twenty-five.

D.S. You must have had some reputation. What in the world would possess a CEO to put a twenty-five-year-old in charge of a gigantic project like that? And did you face any resistance?

D.D. Sure. There was a huge perception issue I had to overcome. I was hired as a product manager and at that time I had no expertise in customer service whatsoever. And here I was working with people who had been in customer service all their lives. And some of them weren't too happy I was there. They were looking at me like, "What is this kid doing here?"

D.S. What was the solution you came up with?

D.D. I used the same approach I have always used ever since then, whenever I have been put in charge of a turnaround position. The first thing I did was listen. At the end of any day, you have to draw your own conclusions. No one else can make your decisions for you. But the first thing you have to do as a manager is you have to go in and listen to a lot of people. And listen to them tell you what they think is wrong. Then you use all of their input to draw your own conclusions and to come up with a plan. And when you draw those conclusions, you have to realize that you can't please everybody. Half the people are going to think you're right, and the other half are going to think you're wrong. And that's where the leadership part takes over.

D.S. How's that?

D.D. You have to have enough confidence to more or less say what you're going to do and let everybody know what the goals are in terms of where you stand today, and what the vision is in terms of where and how you want to grow. And you have to carefully explain to everyone the steps you have to take in order to get there. And you have to honestly let everyone know what the situation is. In this case the situation was bad and so I told them it was bad. I didn't lie to them and tell them everything was perfect, because it wasn't. But I did try to give them a good idea of what the group could do.

D.S. How long did your customer service overhaul take and what were the results that you finally took to the board?

D.D. The initial work took about eighteen months. The results were that, in July 1994, we surpassed IBM in service reliability ratings for a similar data-storage product and had the highest customer satisfaction rating for price as measured by an independent agency.

D.S. That ties in perfectly with the overall theme of this book—that most leading companies do not consider customer service, sales, and marketing to be separate functions, but they are really three corners of the same pyramid. Does that, in fact, describe your own philosophy?

D.D. They are absolutely tied together. When I look at it, and ask myself what made me able to see this service issue in a different light than someone who had been in the business for thirty years, it was that I had just come directly from being a product manager, and had spent on average four days a week in front of customers talking to them. So I was very used to dealing with customers, and used to dealing with them not only on the post-service side but also on the sales side. I know how hard it is to get these products in because they cost about half a million dollars each. And if someone spends a half million dollars on a product and it breaks, and they call you, they want to make sure that they are treated better than they expected. That was my mentality. I wanted to make sure that when people called in with a problem, they left feeling ecstatic, even though they had had a problem.

D.S. What was it about your personality or your behavioral style that caused your CEO, Michael Ruettgers, who has been named by *Business Week* as one of the world's twenty-five best CEOs, to put a twenty-five-year-old in charge of a customer service overhaul for an entire division of your company? What do you think he saw in you that was so special?

D.D. In our product management, we are set up a little differently than other companies. The way our divisions are set up, we got to be our own entrepreneurs. We ran the whole business. We did pricing, we did sales, we did customer communication—everything. We really were running our businesses. So I think that he really did see the management skills that I had. If I was to step back before I started working, I really had been re-hearsing for this role my whole life without knowing it. In college, I was president of my class for four years. I was president of my high school senior class. In all those jobs, in college in particular, I spent a great deal of time with university officials who would invite me into meetings where they were running their business, where they were doing budget reviews, so you really learn a lot. So before I even started, I had learned a lot about the way companies really work. And I was also very used to speaking in public and being articulate. Those are extremely important skills in order to be a successful manager.

D.S. What do you think are the basic traits that allow you to work with people so well?

D.D. On the business level I am confident, but in a quiet way. So I guess you would say I am quietly confident. Also, passion. I am very passionate about what I do. When you take on any project you have to have enough enthusiasm and passion to get everybody who works for you passionate about it. I really believe that people like to be led. They like really strong leaders who can help them get where they want to be.

D.S. How many hours a week do you work, on average?

D.D. Fifty to fifty-five.

D.S. Some people feel you have to work one hundred hours a week in order to be successful. I would gather that you think that is not true.

D.D. If you have to work that many there is something wrong.

D.S. But what about that period in your life when you became so ill, and your friends thought you were going to die?

D.D. What happened was I had added to my fifty-five hours a week at work, thirty-five hours a week at school, so in essence, in the end I had no getaway time. At that time, I was in charge of launching the open systems business here, which was probably the most stressful job I have ever had. . . . I had no down time or rest time, since I was in the high-pressure world of getting an MBA. When I got sick it was the last quarter of the last year I was involved in the MBA program, so I guess I had just pushed myself as far as I could go.

D.S. What did you learn from that experience? What advice would you give to young professionals who want to climb the ladder but not kill themselves at the same time?

D.D. I guess it sounds cliché, but when I got sick, it was a very scary time for me. It was scary not only to be sick, but it was even scarier because they couldn't tell me what was wrong. I went through test after test after test. When you get that sick, everything that you are used to is taken away from you. I could no longer charge with everyone else, when before that I had been constantly go, go, go. My fatigue level was tremendous. And when you get to that point, you ask yourself what's really important. I mean I didn't want to be dead at thirty-two, you know? So how I have changed coming out of that is that I realize I have limits. I think I work smart and I have always worked smart, but now I make sure that I do things outside of work. My weekends are very important to me. I spend time with my fiancée. I spend time doing recreational things, so I can unwind and enjoy myself. The other thing I learned was that the world didn't end because I wasn't there. You can call it maturity or anything you want, but that was the biggest thing I learned. I still work hard, and I still work my fifty-five hours a week, but I don't go above it. I take time to smell the roses now.

D.S. There's a lot of talk these days about the difference between old style management and more enlightened, so-called New Age management styles. Old style says, "You do what I say or you look for another job." New style says, "Let the team lead and you do all you can to minimize fear and hostility in the workplace." Which style works best, in your opinion?

D.D. It completely depends on the situation. If I am brought into a situation where a division is going under and the ship is sinking, I take control. I walk in and say, "Hi, I'm David Donatelli and here's what we're going to do." But in the back of my mind, I'm always planning to turn things over to the team and let the team lead—eventually—once things are straightened out. So I'm always planning for team leadership. . . . But when a division begins to produce, that's when you can begin to let go of the reins. So it's a question of where the organization is. But if you ask me what kinds of organizations are most productive, I would definitely say that it is those organizations that are self-directed.

D.S. Why?

D.D. They have the highest motivation. They also have the greatest job enjoyment. And they are the most creative by far.

D.S. Can you give me an example of an organization that you really admire, from that standpoint, besides your own?

D.D. GE.

D.S. Why?

D.D. I base this on the experience of going to graduate school at Kellogg with GE employees from diverse divisions who had never met each other. It was amazing how they work . . . like a small Silicon Valley start-up. They could all speak a common business language, even though they came from divisions as diverse as GE Capital, to medical devices, to appliances. But they could all talk about the same goals, and the same vision. They all had a sense of entrepreneurial urgency—you know the attitude of "let's take that hill." And there was a feeling of great loyalty because of all the training they had received and all the career growth possibilities they had.

D.S. What impresses you most about GE?

D.D. To have a company that's that big, in terms of not only revenue, but in terms of employees, and to be that diverse, and to have that kind of global understanding of what the company's goals are, and what the company's vision is, and what the mission is, and how they as individuals can contribute to that—I think that's phenomenal.

D.S. How does EMC go about integrating those three functions of sales, marketing, and customer service to its own advantage?

D.D. Service at EMC is not a profit center, which, in this industry, is about 180 degrees away from the norm. Most companies get 30 to 40 percent of their revenues from servicing their products. Our philosophy is really different in that service managers are measured on customer satisfaction—which is measured by outside agencies. Our philosophy is very simple: If we keep our customers happier than anyone else keeps them, in an exploding market like high technology, they are always going to come back and buy more. That is tied directly with sales. Our sales reps get to spend their time finding out customer needs, and then working with the customers and helping them. And they never have to spend their time apologizing that when something went wrong, EMC wasn't there to back them up. So we really feel that we built this simple philosophy into a competitive weapon that has helped us to grow as fast as we have.

D.S. What about the built-in service aspects of your products? Hasn't that set you apart from the pack as well?

D.D. Yes it has. We have actually changed a lot of our products so that if they break or malfunction, they will actually fix themselves. And if they are going to break, the products will call us before they break, so we actually show up at the customer's doorstep—before they even know they're going to have a problem—with the parts ready to fix it. No one else thought about doing that before we started doing it.

D.S. Your company has achieved unparalleled success in its market niche in a remarkably short period of time. How did you achieve it?

D.D. The product that really made us was Symmetrix. We started off in the IBM mainframe data-storage market. In that market, IBM had had the number-one market share for thirty years. At the time, we were a $120 million company with no market share. And we had the audacity, in the minds of some, to think we could come in and take over. So of course a lot of people were looking at us like we had three heads. The way we got around that was by employing just a few basic principles. First, we always delivered more than we committed, which is rare in sales. It's usually just the opposite—you promise the world and deliver half.

D.S. What is your ultimate goal on the service side?

D.D. To overwhelm. We want our customers to be so struck by the difference in the service we provide from the service that the competition provides that they are simply overwhelmed.

D.S. What are some of your strategies to overwhelm the customer, from a service side?

D.D. Innovation is number one. You have to find ways to prevent problems before they occur. You have to spend money in order to be able to do that. Second, if we do detect a problem with any of our services or products, we immediately construct an action plan to take to the customer, and communicate that action plan to the customer immediately, instead of making the customer track us down. Sometimes our plan will be multifaceted. In computers, you often have to have a plan A, plan B, plan C, and a plan D because computer problems are very often not cut-and-dry, or black and white. You often have to try many possible solutions to find one that will work for a particular system. So we are always careful to explain to our customers that if plan A doesn't work, we are going to try plans B, C, and D next. That way, we can help them control their stress level. Because, as you know, computer problems tend to make most people get very stressed out.

D.S. Controlling the customer's stress level—this hits the heart of psychology in salesmanship. The most brilliant experts in business and business psychology have essentially said the same thing. The most important thing you can do is to make your customer feel that you are the knight in shining armor who has come to make her life seem less stressful, because we can assume that most customers feel that everyone else in the world is only there to make their lives seem more stressful.

D.D. Absolutely. But there's another issue, too. The customers who are most loyal to us are the ones who have had something break. Because in computers, something is always going to break eventually. But when something does break, and they see the level of our service, it makes them even more loyal because it gives them peace of mind that they can feel safe with the level of service we will provide, continuously. And that peace of mind is worth a lot of money.

D.S. That's probably the genius of your company from a marketing standpoint, because virtually every computer magazine I have ever read bemoans the horrible lack of service after the sale among most computer products and service companies. Customers get very stressed out and confused—even to the point of tears—but when they need help after the sale, no one seems to care. That's the general feeling you get from reading computer magazines.

D.D. Very true. I guess the word I would use to describe many other companies out there is "indifferent"—just completely indifferent. They don't *care.*

D.S. Not caring is incredibly ignorant, from a psychological point of view. Because, for your corporate buyer, who is incredibly conscientious, nit-picky, and abundantly aware of even the tiniest details, "care" is probably the most imporant word in the language. And people who seem not to care are anathema to them.

D.D. Well, maybe they do care on the inside, but what most computer companies are showing the customer is that they don't seem to care. And that's bad.

D.S. What kind of advertising approaches or slogans do you use to communicate your mission and your level of service?

D.D. I don't think advertising or slogans really work in the computer industry. In this industry, everything is based upon reputation, references, and word-of-mouth recommendations. In this day and age, people are numb to advertising. Our customer base is the global 2,000, most of the largest companies in the world, and they respond to reputation, not ads. If we put an ad out saying we were the greatest thing ever, I don't think anyone would buy that.

D.S. What's your latest project at EMC?

D.D. I have been working on a project for the last year where I am trying to turn around a company that EMC purchased—a start-up software company that does information backup and recovery products. It had some morale problems. In the year I took over, the turnover rate for engineers was in the neighborhood of 55 percent. I have been able to whittle that down to about 7 percent. Before I took over, they were missing all of their release schedules. In my first year, we more or less redid the entire product and achieved 100 percent on-time delivery, with twenty-two releases.

D.S. What were the employees' chief complaints? What were the fundamental problems?

D.D. The employees felt a lack of leadership. They had no idea of what was required of them. Therefore, they weren't meeting any of their goals. And the market was changing and they didn't have a business plan. To use the proverbial expression, they were trying to hug the forest, to be all things to all people. And that doesn't work. What you want with products is something that's distinct, to be known for having one product that's absolutely the best in a certain area of narrow focus. And so that's what we have done. I discontinued development on a number of products that had no relevance to our high-end users. That is, we discontinued all products that had an average selling price of $30,000 and focused more on the products that have an average selling price of $500,000. We decided to focus entirely on the high-end market, because that's where we are most competitive.

D.S. Does the expertise that you bring to this project require a lot of technical knowledge, or are you attacking it more from a marketing- and business-strategy standpoint?

D.D. It's business management, organizational management, and marketing all at the same time. What's interesting about all of my jobs—if you want to know what it's like to "succeed young," so to speak—is that I have gone into each one knowing absolutely nothing about the product or the tasks at hand. For example, in the current task, they asked me to take over the engineering organization and then to manage the whole business. I don't have an engineering degree; I have never worked in engineering in my life. When I took over a manufacturing division earlier in my career, I had no manufacturing experience—I knew nothing about manufacturing. But when I had accomplished my turnaround of that manufacturing division, I was invited to speak at Harvard Business School on the way we do our work—we were able to triple volumes without adding a single person to our head count. So I approach all of my challenges in the same way. It often doesn't matter if you're not a subject matter expert. In fact, in many cases, it often helps not to be. In other words, one of the best things you can have in a manager is a fresh, open mind.

D.S. Almost all of the exceptional corporate leaders that I have had a chance to meet have all had one trait in common—they possess an ability to mind-read their customers, and that's why I titled the book the way I did. How long does this process take, in your opinion? What are the steps?

D.D. You have to spend enough time with your customers to find out what all their requirements for satisfaction are. The one thing that you have to realize about most customers is this: They spend most of their time talking to their colleagues or each other inside a solitary office environment. From a product standpoint, what they lack is a worldview. What you have to do is help bring them the world, come to them and educate them and show them what's going on in their world in terms of the products they could be using and what their options are. Then, you have to find out what their needs and requirements are. Then you put those two things together—what they need, and what the world has to offer—using common sense all the way through the process, and putting the customer's needs first, and letting them know that you are putting their needs first. So, first of all, I would say that you show the customer that you care about his or her world. Then you show them what the rest of the world has to offer. At some point, you hope to show them that your involvement can make their world better—more effective and more efficient. That's really the process that's involved in mind-reading your customers, as far as I can tell. I can't think of a better way to explain it.

CHAPTER 13

A Few More Words about Work, Struggle, and the Real Meaning of Success

A good friend and former associate of mine, Dr. Kurt Luedtke, is a clinical and forensic psychologist. Kurt is a former military psychologist and retired Army Reserve colonel who currently consults with thirty-one police departments and numerous other private and government organizations in addition to the work that we do together.

Although many people, including me, consider Kurt to be one of the most brilliant psychologists they have ever met, many people also consider him to be one of the most eccentric—and so do I.

Whenever Kurt volunteered to drive to a business meeting, I increased my expectations for an interesting ride, because I knew there was a high probability he would show up in his canary yellow 1966 souped-up Chevelle with a 427 under the hood, a B&M Powerglide transmission, seven coats of competition paint, center-line drag wheels, a 373 Positraction rear end, and a Crane Saturday Night Special Racing Cam with a 586 lift. Not your standard business mobile by any means, but a car that is guaranteed to have superior traction and maneuverability.

Needless to say, Kurt is not a restrained psychologist, nor does he claim to be. But in terms of helping his patients and his organizational development clients to achieve greater focus, happiness, and productivity, I have met very few people who are equal to him in his field.

I knew that I wanted to work with Kurt when I first heard him explain his technique in marriage counseling. Far and wide, he is known as one of the most effective marriage counselors in North Carolina, so one day before we became partners I asked him what his secret was.

"The approach that I use, for lack of a better expression, might be called a Judeo-Christian and/or spiritual approach," he said. "When people come to me for help with their marriage, and it looks like divorce is imminent, I make a simple proposition. I say: 'I will help you save your marriage, but first I want you to make a commitment, too. I want you to try and make a commitment to a spiritual lifestyle. By this I mean the following: I want you to try your best to be nice to other people, including your spouse, each and every day. I want you to forgive other people their faults and weaknesses, including your spouse's weaknesses and your own weaknesses. I want you to go out of your way to be kind and tolerant to everyone you meet. And to the best of your ability, I want you to try to stop doing things that you know are wrong and just live the right way, as your conscience dictates. Do you think you can do that for me?'

"If people tell me, 'No, I'm sorry I can't do that,' then I tell them that I simply can't help them at all," Luedtke said. "At that point I suggest they seek another therapist. Many of them do. Sometimes they go to these counselors who want to see them for two years. They go by the textbook and avoid the spiritual side of life. They work on 'negotiating' *issues* and drawing up a list of emotional demands. It's all very intellectual and self-centered. And it doesn't work. And it costs a lot of money. So eventually, these people will come right back to the brink of divorce and many of them will eventually come back and say, 'Okay, fine, we're ready to kill each other. Let me hear about the religious therapy again. I guess we'll try it.' And if they do, it usually saves their marriage. It's the only thing that works, in my experience. And I can get my clients back on the road to happiness in a few months or less if they'll follow this approach."

When Kurt finished this explanation, I recognized a kindred soul, and it was in that moment that I knew we would probably become a team in our organizational development work. His suggestions were very helpful to me in my formative years as a consultant.

I also think that many of Kurt's theories on achieving focus and managing anxiety in the workplace have phenomenal importance for those of us who have been trying to be aggressive and successful and competitive without being eaten alive by stress.

The tentative title of a new book that I am working on is *How to Stay Competitive without Losing Your Soul.* Staying competitive and energetic without becoming a monster is a tricky process by most people's estimation. So I think it's a very important theme. How, in fact, do you maintain a proper level of aggressiveness and chutzpah without allowing the darker forces of competition to erode your sense of respect for yourself and your peace of mind?

Although we don't have time to explore that issue completely in this book, we can preface it here with a few of the observations I have gleaned from Kurt, and one of my other consulting advisers, David Amsellem, M.D., a distinguished psychiatrist.

In terms of maximizing your performance and managing anxiety and stress in the workplace, these are the concepts I believe are most fundamental:

1. Human beings are capable of unlimited performance as long as they are treated with respect.

2. Psychological health is maximized when people strive to be kind, calm, and respectful under all circumstances.

3. Mental clarity and decision making are maximized when human beings are calm.

4. It is impossible for human beings to remain calm and mentally clear when work environments allow hostility, superiority, disrespect, or arrogance in any form.

5. The way human beings talk to one another, for better or worse, is the single greatest predictor of psychological health or illness.

With these points in mind, I thought you might find it interesting to hear how Luedtke, a psychologist, and Amsellem, a psychiatrist, perceive the cause of anxiety in the workplace, and in our individual lives. I thought you would also be interested to hear how they believe we can eliminate much unnecessary anxiety by maintaining our focus and our faith, whatever our personal belief systems might be.

D.S. Kurt, you are a counselor for numerous private and governmental organizations and hundreds of individual clients. What percentage of your patients come in for disorders that are primarily related to anxiety?

K.L. Between 75 and 80 percent.

D.S. Can you give us an example of what some of those anxiety-related disorders might be?

K.L. From diagnostic criteria, we know that about 25 percent of the population suffer from an anxiety disorder at any given time. That might be a generalized anxiety disorder. It might be posttraumatic stress disorder. It might be something as simple as an adjustment disorder with anxiety. But I think anxiety is more complicated than just the expression of symptoms. It's a matter of personal philosophy. It's a matter of life planning, in some ways. And it certainly involves your definition of success in the professional world.

D.S. Do you think that anxiety often stems from simple causes, despite its complexity?

K.L. Sure, in many cases I would say that it does. If you are looking for a synonym for anxiety, it is conflict. Basically many of us want to have it all, but we don't want to sacrifice anything, in any way, shape, or form. It's like the old story of the monkey that reached his hand into the cage to grab the nut. The nut is fastened to the floor and won't move but the monkey won't let go of the nut and ends up being captured. In many ways, there are an awful lot of us who just won't let go of that nut.

D.S. In earlier parts of this book, I have talked about the importance of staying on the board—adhering to your values and your mission—as a way of maintaining a sense of peace and purpose. Do you feel that when people are off the board, so to speak, that that contributes to anxiety?

K.L. I look at these issues from a theological/spiritual perspective. The farther you stray from the manufacturer's instructions with regard to operating the human being, the more likely you are to have problems with yourself. I think our manufacturer is God, and God has given us a set of instructions to live by, certain guidelines. For people of varying religions, these guidelines are often to be found in the texts of the major religious faiths. As a Christian, the guidebook I tend to refer to is the Holy Bible. I consider it a major portion of the manufacturer's handbook. If the commandments are lived by, people will have few problems compared with a life outside of the commandments. The more one strays from the manufacturer's instructions, the more conflict occurs and accrues in that person's life.

D.S. David Amsellem, as a psychiatrist with an M.D., how would you handle the same question?

D.A. I have a slightly different perspective. Life in the twentieth century is very different than it was two or three hundred years ago. Everything is more complicated. Relationships are very complex. People tend to live apart. There is more divorce. Parents have children living in all different parts of the country. Because of the increasing separation among people, many people are finding that their basic human emotional needs are not being met. In the past, there was a lot of community interaction. These days, people are too busy to talk to their neighbors. People are too busy for their children, their spouses, their families. People are so starved for both physical love and affection that they often find themselves becoming involved in relationships that are destructive.

K.L. I think we are on the same page, Dr. Amsellem and I. I think we're talking about the issue of love. A lot of people say God is love and I think that is important when you look at the sense of separation that people feel in the world today. For example, consider the pain that a child feels if it thinks that it is not loved by its father. Then think about our relation to God. I think the ultimate loss of self-esteem comes when we don't realize that we are all children of God and that we are absolutely cast in the image of God.

D.S. Okay, so a patient comes to you and says that he or she is feeling anxiety, and describes a lifestyle that seems to be "off of the board," so to speak, where do you start, in terms of trying to help that person, especially when they seem to be completely confused about the cause of their pain?

D.A. I use an interpersonal approach, and I try to communicate the idea of respect. I try to get my patients to understand that they are worth respect, they are worth love, and they are worth dignity, and so they shouldn't try to lose all of that by giving themselves over to things that are destructive, whatever it is—a destructive relationship, alcohol, or anything else. I try to teach them that it is better to seek fulfillment with other people in healthy relationships, and to work toward becoming self-reliant at the same time.

D.S. A lot of the seminars that we are conducting have to do with the idea that you can become more focused and successful in your professional endeavors by becoming more focused in a spiritual sense as well. How do the two of you view this process, from your different theoretical perspectives?

D.A. I use a developmental approach, and when you speak of a developmental approach, you are not speaking of children only. I try to get people to understand what stage of life they are in, where they are in terms of where they want to be.

K.L. I think when you look at life and success and struggle and conflict, the first thing you have to come to grips with is *why*? Why are we here? What's the raison d'être, as the French say. Well, I am fairly well certain the reason we're here is not to be customers for Charmin toilet tissue, and the reason for being here is not to buy Range Rovers, or even '66 Chevelles. I think that the reason we are here on earth is to pass a series of tests. I like the expression used by M. Scott Peck, who calls our existence here on earth a kind of "celestial boot camp." I love that expression and I wish I had thought of it first. But I also think that when we spend our time here on earth trying to better ourselves, while simultaneously following the instructions of our creator in our business lives and in our personal lives, that we have actually enrolled ourselves in a management-training program for eternity. We are preparing ourselves to have that eventual meeting with God, the CEO of the universe.

D.S. What is one of the first conditions that must be met in order to pass these tests?

K.L. First of all, to be real. There is so much phoniness in our society today. There are a few people out there who understand that if you want to have a degree from a good school, you have to work hard, get into the school, and then graduate. Most people these days would rather go out and find a place to buy a fake degree and hang it on their walls, just for the image, the same way they would buy a fake Rolex. Here in North Carolina, our state motto is "To be rather than to seem," but in so many segments of our society today the motto is "To seem rather than to be." It's time for a reality check. If you want to be successful, learn to teach people to expect that you will do what you say you'll do, and that you say what you mean and mean what you say. It's really that simple.

D.S. As you know, there is a huge undercurrent in most major corporate environments that is a backlash against phoniness. In the eighties and early nineties, it was very important to seem like you were important. Now there's a huge trend toward hiring people who are soft-spoken, capable, and humble. I can't tell you how many successful young executives have told me that the day of the arrogant egomaniac is winding to a close. What do you make of this trend?

D.A. There is a new consciousness that is evolving, and I think it is a consciousness of altruism. People have begun to realize that what they want is to fulfill basic human needs that can't be fulfilled by material possessions alone. I understand why the climate in the business world is changing, and all over society. It's because people are realizing that just owning an Armani suit or a Rolls Royce doesn't fulfill any basic human need. What people need is self-esteem. And they need community. They need to give. They need to help others. What we are seeing is just the beginning of a new consciousness.

D.S. So maybe the anxiety that a lot of us in the business world feel from time to time is important. Maybe it's like a wake-up call.

K.L. It is. That's exactly what it is. Anxiety is your friend. Anxiety is your teacher. It's one of the best mentors you'll ever have. Sometimes anxiety is there to teach us lessons about what is really important in life and what is not. And along these lines, there is a quote that I have always liked. It says, "It is nice to be important, but it is more important to be nice." Sometimes, the recognition of that concept alone goes a long way to helping us get our heads on straight.

D.A. I agree completely. Finding true success in life is often about learning the benefits of kindness. There is a therapeutic benefit in learning to be kind.

D.S. So from your diverse perspectives, let's take a look at what the two of you would consider to be the "secret of life," in terms of getting along better with others, finding inner peace, and being more successful in your chosen careers. What do you think?

K.L. I would like to address this from my personal point of view, and this comes from living a wide and varied and energetic life and learning a lot of lessons the hard way. I certainly think the key to happiness is faith and devotion to spiritual beliefs. I certainly recognize the importance of anyone's personal belief system, but I will speak of my own belief system, which is Christianity. As a Christian, I fundamentally believe that the secret to success involves doing your best to follow the teachings of the Lord, while at the same time keeping your feet planted firmly on the board, and never straying from the missions and values that you know to be right. I could go on and on, and describe the various bits and pieces of my philosophy, but I really don't think that I can put it more succinctly than that. Some people would say that I am a flagrant Christian, or a flaming Christian, but I don't think I'm even worthy of that term. I guess that you can say that I am simply an aspiring Christian. I want to be one, so I do my best every day to come nearer to that goal. These days and times, our society seems not to want to play by the rules, but to constantly bend the rules in order to accommodate our behavior. I think that as we understand the meaning of this new consciousness that Dr. Amsellem has described, we will begin to find that it is much more important to amend our behavior to fit the rules.

D.A. For me, if I can touch the lives of the people I meet in a positive way, at any level, then I can say that I have had a good day. That's it. That's all I can say about the meaning of success.

Epilogue

One of the things that excites me the most about the future is the enormous opportunity for growth and happiness each and every one of us shares, especially as we learn to create more opportunities together through collaborative networking.

The process of writing this book has been fun for me because as I was writing it, I mailed it out in stages to businesspeople across the United States for their feedback, and in many instances, people wanted to get involved with the message of the book—the ultimate message of helping others.

I find this inspiring because I have spoken with hundreds of businesspeople in high places during the completion of this book, and almost everyone is saying the following:

- The new millennium is going to be fun.

- Arrogant blowhards in the business world are *really* beginning to annoy most real business leaders.

- Hypocrites and phonies are getting more pink slips.

- Spirituality and values are back and here to stay.

- Successful people who are nice people are banding together for strength.

- There's a war going on in the business world between nice people and mean people, and the mean people are losing.

As a way of capitalizing on the opportunity for making positive changes in the way we all work together, live together, and treat one another, many experts from both my home city of Goldsboro, North Carolina, and other parts of the state and nation—experts who include some nationally recognized psychologists and physicians—have been very helpful in advising me as I created programs to research and address these issues.

I have organized my consulting practice around one principal idea: I am convinced that much of the pathology, misery, sadness, depression, and anxiety existing in the world today—conditions that lead to substance abuse, personal agony, and visits to doctors and therapists—are created by unhealthy work environments, that is to say, environments in which people are allowed to be hostile or rude to one another.

My personal lifetime goal is to do whatever I can to help teach organizations that companies that require employees to treat one another with respect are the most competitive companies.

Companies that enforce rules of conduct to create healthy, respectful work environments are also companies with lower health-care expenditures for employment-related anxiety disorders, I would wager, and I also bet these companies have more productive and creative employees as well.

I have a hunch that my colleagues and I are going to be working on this one simple message for the rest of our lives, the world being the way it is. But, if you have any good ideas as to how we can accomplish the goal more effectively, please write to me at the e-mail address listed on page 199.

Finding Gold in Your Own Backyard

There's one more thing I would like to say:

You don't have to live in a big city these days in order to be "successful." Of course, success means many different things to different people. So, I will allow a broad definition that defines success as having the opportunity to work with people you respect, and to respect the work you are able to do with other people, while using your God-given talents to the fullest to fulfill your own personal definition of a meaningful life.

But no matter how you slice it, one thing is clear: No matter *what* you want to do, recent advances in information technology have made it possible for almost anyone, anywhere in the world, to be a "player." As virtual offices and virtual education become the norm, the only thing that will really determine the full achievement of your hopes and dreams will be the level of your drive, commitment, and imagination. That is, most leading experts on the future concede that almost anyone from any hamlet on the globe can be a successful businessperson these days—because of the advances in technology.

All of that is simply to say I want to highly encourage you to follow your own dreams no matter where you are or what you happen to be doing.

It would not be a wise business move to let anyone diminish your faith in your own ingenuity or potential. We all have our areas of brilliance and promise, every one of us, and all we have to do to achieve happiness and success is to stay focused and to stand up for our dreams.

And help one another when we can.

That's what this book was supposed to be about—and I hope the message came through.

Ultimately, I really wanted to talk about the beneficial aspects of togetherness.

Because in the end, as you know, a spirit of togetherness makes for very good business.

A Brief History of the DISC Behavioral Methodology and Competing DISC Products

As I mentioned earlier, the DISC methodology of analyzing behavioral styles is largely based upon the work of a Harvard psychologist named William Moulton Marston, who published a book titled *Emotions of Normal People* in 1928.

Marston's work was not very well recognized or acknowledged in his own lifetime, and his theories did not find a popular audience until they were revised and expanded upon by various psychologists and researchers beginning in the 1950s. Since that time, a wealth of diagnostic instruments and training tools using the DISC system have been developed by independent and competing companies specializing in creating behavioral training tools for the workplace.

For companies interested in procuring DISC-based training products for their own teams, I should make it clear that there are several companies that manufacture slightly different versions of diagnostic and training tools that examine the DISC dimensions of drive, influencing ability, steadfastness, and conscientiousness.

If you were to place telephone calls to these individual companies, the owners of these competing products would tell you that their tools were vastly superior to all other tools on the market and more accurate, too. This, of course, is a natural sentiment for genuine competitors to have in a competitive marketplace. If you don't think your products are superior, you probably shouldn't be in business in the first place.

From my own personal point of view, however—and I have examined several different varieties of DISC instruments from competing companies—it seems that the competing companies offer products that are simply better for different purposes, depending on what you need, and the price you feel you can afford.

So, in an effort to be fair and neutral, I will simply list the addresses of the companies that I know offer validated versions of DISC scoring instruments.

If you are interested in learning more about the history of DISC, or purchasing DISC-based products, call the companies listed below and ask them to send you literature about the products, and then compare the products and prices in light of your own needs.

From my point of view, I have found that the DISC inventories, when used to give you a sense of your own behavioral style, are most useful as a discussion tool. I firmly believe, as I have said many times, that your *own impression* of your behavioral strengths and weaknesses is much more valid and important than any information or reading that any tool can give you.

But if you are a corporate customer, and you are interested in exploring all of the different DISC-based training tools out there, you can contact me and I'll give you my own two cents worth of additional advice.

And if there are any other companies offering DISC-based products whose names I have not mentioned (perhaps some have sprung up since this book went to press), I sincerely apologize.

However, I think that if you went on the Internet and typed in either "DISC" or "DiSC" (the Carlson Learning Group uses that acronym), you will probably find just about everything about available DISC products you need to know.

One company manufacturing a popular line of DISC products (including software products) is TTI Performance Systems, Ltd., based in Scottsdale, Arizona. The company's president, Bill Bonnstetter, has been very helpful as I have prepared this book. He has called on many occasions and spoken to me at length about the history of the DISC. He also has been unusually fair, in my opinion, in discussing the contributions and importance of the work of his competitors in advancing the development of DISC-based tools, an attitude that is sometimes rare in the business world today. (Also, Bonnstetter read the original draft of this book from cover to cover in order to give me some feedback based on his decades of experience as a sales psychology researcher, and I greatly appreciate that.) Because Bonnstetter has been so helpful, I have invited him to contribute a few paragraphs describing the history of the DISC in his own words, fully appreciating that some of his competitors might have a different perspective on how the diagnostic instrument has evolved.

Again, this information from Bonnstetter is offered only as a general overview for insatiably curious readers, and I value his viewpoint simply because he has been extremely helpful to me. But if you are a truly curious soul, I advise you to contact the leaders of the other companies listed on page 193, who will probably give you their own version of the history of the DISC.

A History of the DISC, by Bill Bonnstetter, President, TTI Performance Systems, Ltd.

In his 1928 book, *Emotions of Normal People,* William Moulton Marston defined four dimensions of each person. The people he studied varied in their intensity of these dimensions and therefore exhibited different behavior patterns.

Marston went on to teach at Columbia University, and there he directed the master's thesis of a student named Walter Clarke, who produced a paper titled "Physical Types as a Basis for Variations in Primary Emotions." Upon graduation, Clarke used the concept to select employees. He found the performance level of certain jobs correlated to the dimensions Marston had outlined.

Clarke then went on to validate a questionnaire called the Activity Vector Analysis (AVA) and, in 1948, established his own company to publish the AVA, providing the necessary training to those who wanted to use the questionnaire.

A number of people employed at the Walter Clarke company left and designed their own questionnaires similar to the AVA. This has resulted in a number of questionnaires being developed to measure the four dimensions identified by Marston.

In the 1950s, J. P. Cleaver added significant improvements to the system. He changed the graph from horizontal to vertical, making it easier to read and interpret (see David Snyder's style analysis graphs in Appendix B for an example). Cleaver also grouped the responses into groups of four, forcing people to choose what they were most or least like. Most DISC companies in the marketplace today have followed the works of J. P. Cleaver.

In the 1970s, John Geier designed the first self-scoring questionnaire and added more responses to the instrument so people could respond and get feedback in one session. Geier later sold his company to Kirk Carlson, and today the instrument is marketed by Carlson Learning.

In the 1980s, Bill Bonnstetter, with Target Training International, Ltd., researched the buying style of farmers and validated that the appearance of a farmer's farmstead correlated with Marston's DISC dimensions. He developed a sales training program called Buyer Profile Blending, which trains salespeople how to identify the buying style of a farmer before they actually meet with him. Additional research proved his concept could be used to train all outside salespeople to read the physical appearance of businesses and offices. This sales training continues to get results in all fields.

In 1984, Bonnstetter and John Hall validated Marston's concept in the selection of over-the-road truck drivers. To eliminate the labor-intensive part of analyzing a graph, the process was computerized. TTI used its research from the farmers and truck drivers along with other research to expand the reports into other fields.

DISC (or DiSC) Product Suppliers

AMACOM Books
P.O. Box 169
Saranac Lake, NY 12983
Tel.: 800-714-6395
Fax: 518-891-3653

TTI Performance Systems, Ltd.
16020 N. 77th Street
Scottsdale, AZ 85260
Tel.: 480-443-1077
Fax: 480-443-0163
E-mail: http://www.ttidisc.com

Geier Learning Systems
10650 County Road 81, Suite 103
Maple Grove, MN 55369
Tel.: 763-493-3374
Fax: 763-677-3090

Inscape Publishing
6465 Wayzata Boulevard
Suite 800
Minneapolis, MN 55426
Tel.: 763-765-2222
Fax: 763-765-2277

David Snyder's DISC Style Analysis Graphs

The graphs on page 197 give an example of how the DISC is used to interpret and predict behavior. I have used my own as examples since I have tried to make a clean breast of my own strengths and weaknesses in the course of this book.

These particular graphs are based upon an inexpensive paper and pencil self-scoring instrument developed by TTI Performance Systems. I entered the data from this instrument into a computer program also designed by TTI and produced the graphs, which perfectly describe my behavior, and the way I have adopted my behavior to the workplace—for better or for worse.

Graph number II is called the Basic Style. Generally speaking, it shows how I was born—a guy with a lot of drive who was pretty friendly as well. You can tell this by looking at the high plotting points for drive and influencing ability on Graph II.

Graph I is my adapted style, which shows what happened to me when I entered the workplace. I lost a lot of my friendliness, I think, during working years when I put myself under way too much stress in an effort to achieve goals that I felt were important. That currently represents my weakness—and I work on it every day. I have got to learn how to relax a lot more, and to temper my drive, while putting a lot more emphasis on recapturing my old friendly side.

What people seem to like most about me—in the business world and in the social world—is not my ambition, but my people skills.

As I have mentioned many times over, I think it behooves all salespeople to take a good hard look at their strengths and weaknesses, because if we do not recognize them and face them for what they are, we will never be as successful as we can be.

Any corporate leaders who would like to learn more about the various training tools available that can help sales and marketing people recognize and deal with their individual strengths and weaknesses can feel free to contact me via the e-mail address provided on page 199.

STYLE ANALYSIS GRAPHS

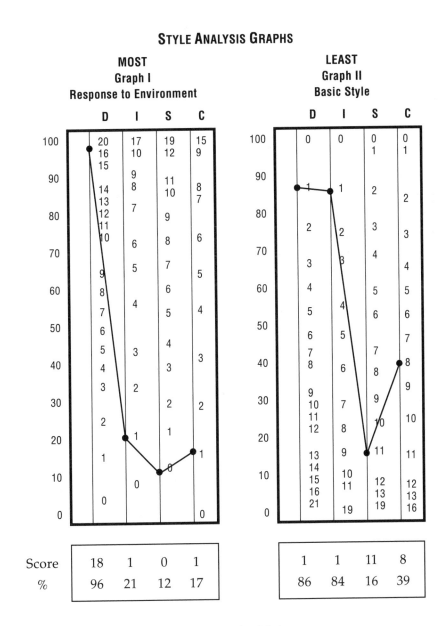

MOST
Graph I
Response to Environment

LEAST
Graph II
Basic Style

Copyright © 1984–1997, Target Training International, Ltd.

How to Contact David Snyder and His Associates

Drawing from all of the information in this book, as well as other sources, my colleagues and I do training programs and large-scale organizational consulting programs to help small and large businesses alike accentuate teamwork and drive, along with increased sales and marketing effectiveness, while building a better public image in terms of likeability, conscientiousness, and steadfastness.

To contact us for a private and confidential consultation, please e-mail me at dsnyder@mindread.net. You can also visit our web site at www.mindread.net.

Suggested Reading

The following works have been used as both references and philosophical "guides" in the writing of this book. I would recommend most of them simply because they are each fascinating and extremely well-written works.

They are listed according to their general subject heading. While they certainly do not represent every book that has been written on these subjects (many other ones are out there, I can assure you), they do represent some of my favorites.

The Future of Business

Covey, Stephen. *The 7 Habits of Highly Effective People* (New York: Fireside, 1990). Since everyone with a job has this book now, it can't help but shape the future of organizational development. So you have to read it if you haven't already, especially if you want to buck the system and make up your own book.

Ewing, David W. *Inside the Harvard Business School: Strategies and Lessons of America's Leading School of Business* (New York: Random House, 1990). Clearly identifies the top trends and subject areas that have created the intellectual agenda of Harvard Business School.

Hamel, Gary, and C. K. Prahalad. *Competing for the Future* (Boston: The Harvard Business School Press, 1994). One of the best books available on strategic planning and the quest for competitiveness.

Rosen, Anita. *The E-Commerce Question and Answer Book* (New York: Amacom, 2000). Answers the most commonly posed questions, on how to enter the future world of business.

Marketing/Customer Service

Adler, Stan. *The Zen of Selling* (New York, Amacom, 1998).

Anderson, Kristin, and Ron Zemke. *Delivering Knock Your Socks Off Service*, rev. ed. (AMACOM: New York, 1998).

Donnelly, James H., Jr. *Close to the Customer: 25 Management Tips from the Other Side of the Counter* (Homewood, IL: Business One Irwin, 1992).

Lash, Linda M. *The Complete Guide to Customer Service* (New York: John Wiley & Sons, 1989).

Lele, Milind M. with Jagdish N. Sheth. *The Customer Is Key: Gaining an Unbeatable Advantage through Customer Satisfaction* (New York: John Wiley & Sons, 1987).

Levinson, Jay, and Seth Godin. *The Guerilla Marketing Handbook* (New York: Houghton Mifflin, 1994). Practical and comprehensive tips for trench-level marketing. Good stuff.

Misner, Ivan R. *The World's Best-Known Marketing Secret: Word of Mouth Marketing* (Austin, TX: Bard & Stephen, 1994).

Treacy, Michael, and Fred Wiersema. *The Discipline of Market Leaders: Choose Your Customers, Narrow Your Focus, Dominate Your Market* (New York: Addison-Wesley, 1995).

Zemke, Ron, and Tom Connellan. *E-Service: 24 Ways to Keep Your Customers When the Competition Is Just a Click Away* (AMACOM: New York, 2001).

Creativity

Cameron, Julia. *The Artist's Way* (New York: Tarcher/Putnam, 1992). A great book for all of us who want to tell our inner and outer critics how and why they should go to Hades. Then, great tips for stimulating our creative side.

Siler, Todd. *Think Like a Genius* (New York: Bantam Books, 1997).

Stress Management and Corporate Wellness

Benson, Herbert, M.D., and Eileen Stuart. *The Wellness Book: The Comprehensive Guide to Maintaining Health and Treating Stress-*

Related Illness (Secaucus, NJ: Carol Publishing Group, 1992). The best overview of personal health management that I have read, written by the nation's top wellness experts from the leading center of wellness research.

Goleman, Daniel, Ph.D., and Joel Gurin. *Mind/Body Medicine: How to Use Your Mind for Better Health* (Yonkers, NY: Consumer Reports Books, 1993).

Philosophy/Science

Becker, Ernest. *The Denial of Death* (New York: Free Press, 1973). A Pulitzer Prize–winning masterpiece. Gave me more insight into my pet peeves, fears, self-defeating thoughts, and the reasons for my occasional human outbursts of illogical, nonproductive mortal angst than any other book I have read so far. Reminded me that every person who has ever achieved anything great went insane at least once for a brief period as he or she made that critical break with the status quo.

Benson, Herbert, M.D. *Your Maximum Mind* (New York: Random House, 1987). Another great one from Herbert Benson, with Miriam Z. Klyper, that goes beyond his classic work, *The Relaxation Response* (New York: William Morrow, 1975) to describe techniques that can be used to achieve greater mental energy and focus.

Capra, Fritjof. *The Tao of Physics* (New York: Bantam, 1977). Makes your mind and your soul tingly all at once. Reminds you that there is more harmony and order in the universe than you would ever be able to image even if your brain was 4 million times larger than it is now.

Hobson, Allan, J., M.D. *The Chemistry of Conscious States* (New York: Little, Brown and Company, 1994). From Harvard Medical School's famous dream researcher. Offers a fascinating glimpse of the nature of consciousness and predicts the future of research into human behavior.

Moore, Thomas. *Care of the Soul* (New York: HarperCollins, 1992). An excellent work for monitoring the progress of your inner life and the health of your spirit. Reminds you that truly creative people are not afraid of social mores and/or critics and more or less do what their souls lead them to do. Conversely, it will probably help you to remember that all of those people out there who sit back and criticize achievers like you are probably frightened, self-righteous, and envious of your independence.

Norick, Robert. *The Examined Life* (New York: Simon & Schuster, 1989). An excellent collection of easy to read but eloquent essays about the things that really matter in life, and how to get your head on straight.

Trends

Cornish, Edward, ed. *Exploring Your Future* (Bethesda, MD: World Future Society). Just about everything you want to know about the future of everything from networking, to virtual organizations, to the top-ten technologies for the next ten years, plus an introduction to the greatest thinkers and books that address these themes. Worth its weight in platinum.

Howard, Philip K. *The Death of Common Sense* (New York: Random House, 1994). Reminds us that if we don't want meddlesome, bumbling lawyers and politicians to completely ruin our lives, we have to get politically active and stop them from doing the stupid things they do while all of us businesspeople are looking the other way.

Patterson, James, and Peter Kim. *The Day America Told the Truth* (New York: Prentice-Hall Press, 1991). Absolutely terrifying. An eyeball-opening book coauthored by the J. Walter Thompson advertising agency chairman who polled America on its habits and values. Will scare you to death.

Popcorn, Faith. *The Popcorn Report* (New York: Doubleday, 1991). Faith Popcorn holds forth on the future of your company, your world, and your life. Most of the important consumer trends are in here.

Humor

Adams, Scott. *The Dilbert Principle* (New York: HarperCollins, 1996). The last word on corporate humor, as everyone knows by now.

Psychology

Bonnstetter, Bill J., Judy I. Suiter, and Randy Widrick. *The Universal Language of DISC: A Reference Manual* (Scottsdale, AZ: Target Training International, 1993). An extremely useful and practical book on how to use behavioral psychology to improve success in the workplace.

Hunt, Morton. *The Story of Psychology* (New York: Doubleday, 1993). An excellent and highly readable overview of the people and theories that revolutionized our understanding of human personality and behavior.

Nicholi, Armand M., Jr., M.D., ed. *The New Harvard Guide to Psychiatry* (Cambridge, MA: Harvard University Press, 1988). Everything you always wanted to know about your psyche, your fears, your problems, and the annoying or psychotic behavior patterns of those around you. Suggestions on what can be done and what has to be tolerated.

Ostrander, Sheila, and Lynn Schroeder. *Super-Learning* (New York: Dell, 1982). Some great tips on how to improve your learning skills and ability to memorize.

Sullivan, Henry Stack, M.D. *The Interpersonal Theory of Psychiatry* (New York: W.W. Norton & Company, 1953). An amazing, helpful, and trendsetting book about the way our interpersonal relationships shape our lives, our health, and our success. Still wonderful after all these years.

How to Improve Communication Skills

McKay, Matthew, Ph.D., Martha Davis, Ph.D., and Patrick Fanning. *The Communication Book* (Oakland, CA: New Harbinger Publications, 1983). Comprehensively practical text for improving your communications skills with other human beings.

Solomon, Muriel. *Working with Difficult People* (Englewood Cliffs, NJ: Prentice Hall, 1990). Useful tips for dealing with a range of annoying behavioral types in the workplace and how to diffuse their ability to undermine your own efforts.

History/General Knowledge

Hart, Michael. *The 100: A Ranking of the Most Influential People in History* (Secaucus, NJ: Carol Publishing Group, 1989). An excellent read on how some of history's most influential leaders left their mark, oftentimes by getting other people to do what they wanted them to. Reminds you that inside every great leader there's a great salesman.

Jones, Judy, and William Wilson. *An Incomplete Education* (New York: Random House, 1987). Everything you should have learned in college but probably didn't or forgot. A masterpiece of elucidation, sarcasm, scathing wit, knowledge, trivia, and humor.

Spirituality

Tickle, Phyllis. *God-Talk in America* (New York: Crossroad Publishing Company, 1997). A controversial book, described as both profound and superficial, according to which reviewer you are reading. I think it is an immensely intelligent and well-researched book that gives more practical facts about the reasons behind the growing interest in spirituality in America than anything I have read in a long, long time. You need to know what your customers are thinking about spirituality, so I highly recommend this read.

Index